My Purpose Driven Life:

The Best for the Last

by

Rev. Dr. Margaret Jean Howard

DORRANCE PUBLISHING CO
EST. 1920
PITTSBURGH, PENNSYLVANIA 15238

Dorrance Publishing Co
585 Alpha Drive
Pittsburgh, PA 15238
Visit our website at *www.dorrancebookstore.com*

ISBN: 978-1-6470-2501-4
eISBN: 978-1-6470-2722-3

I dedicate this book to my parents, Jacob C. and Bernice Williams, and to my daughter, Angela Dionne Fernandes. Because of them, I am me.

Contents

Foreword . . . .*vii*

Chapter 1 . . . .*1*
Growing up in Sweet Home Alabama

Chapter 2 . . . .*54*
The Reality of Being Poor in a Big City

Chapter 3 . . . .*65*
My Fears and Struggles

Chapter 4 . . . .*107*
Believing in Myself Against the Odds

Chapter 5 . . . .*157*
The Valleys and the Mountain Tops

Chapter 6 . . . .*191*
A New Beginning

Chapter 7 . . . .*211*
I Remain a Work in Progress

Foreword

Train a child in the way she/he should go, and when she/he is old, she/he will not depart from it (Proverbs 22:6, King James Version).

I was taught and believed that all good things were possible if I worked very hard and held on to God's unchanging hand. To some, this may appear naïve and even ridiculous. But it worked for me. Hard work has never frightened me, and I have grown accustomed to it. Working hard to achieve my goals was a way of life that I learned from my parents and all of the successful people I admired. I grew up believing my achievements would be appreciated much more if I worked hard for them. And all of the people I loved and admired had achieved their successes through their hard work.

I am a descendent of enslaved Africans and African Americans, the daughter of fourth and fifth grade educated parents whose primary source of income was from sharecropping. According to my family's oral history, which has been passed from one generation to another, my paternal grandfather, Henry Williams, was born in slavery. After the Civil War, his former slave master taught him to read and write. My paternal grandfather was ten-years-old when all of this occurred and lived in Georgia at that time.

As a young man, my paternal grandfather married his first wife and fathered five children. His first wife died while the children were still very young, and my paternal grandfather arranged for relatives to raise his five children as their own. Afterwards, my paternal grandfather moved to Abbeville, Alabama, where he met and married my paternal grandmother, Mandy Kelly. Papa Henry and Grandma Mandy had 13 children. Dad was the third youngest son.

Papa Henry was a sharecropper and a pastor of a couple of small churches in Alabama. He traveled from church to church each month, and my uncles and aunts were responsible for working the farm in his absence.

At the age of 12, Daddy asked permission from Papa Henry to quit school and to allow his sisters to attend school full-time. Daddy did this so that his sisters would not have to continue performing those heavy chores required of them. Daddy convinced his father that he was much stronger and could out perform all of his sisters on a daily basis. He promised his father that his sisters would teach him everything they had learned in school in the evenings after supper. Papa Henry gave his permission, and that is why Daddy had a fourth grade formal education.

In regards to Mama, she was adopted at the age of three weeks. Her birth mother named Mama Margaret. During the adoption process, mama's new parents changed her name to Bernice. My maternal grandmother and my maternal grandfather were childless until they adopted Mama. By the time they officially became parents of a three-week-old baby girl, they were considered an older couple back in the day and even possibly by today's standards. Mama told me that her mother and father spoiled her with lots of love and indulged her in everything she wanted. When Mama expressed her desire to quit school, her parents gave their consent. Mama had a fifth grade formal education.

When Mama married Daddy, she did not know how to cook and wash clothes. Daddy was almost ten years older than Mama, which meant that he was 26 and mama was 16, according to their marriage date that was recorded in the family Bible.

Although my maternal and parental grandparents and parents had very little formal education, all of them emphasized the importance of obtaining as much formal education as possible and of accepting Jesus Christ as my Lord and Savior. Primarily, the teachers were the only people I heard speaking correct English during the first 17 years of my life. Nevertheless, I managed to obtain five college degrees in my lifetime and a certificate in Ministry.

There are life's lessons I learned at a very young age, which have helped me to remain focused and work through the most challenging situations. If I included every one of them, my first book probably would be far too depressing. Although I attempted to write my first book when I was in my twenties, there was much work remaining for me to complete and many years of experiences that hindered my first attempt. I've lived many decades since then, and now I have the time and freedom to share my life's journey without hesitation. This is my story.

Acknowledgments

I thank my sister, Dr. Cassie Luke, who has always been supportive of me and remains my best friend and confidant. Thanks to my husband, Robert Howard, who fell in love with me at first glance and remains the love of my life. My gratitude goes to my son, Robert Howard Jr., who encouraged me to write this book several years ago so that my story would be told accurately and well documented. Thanks to my professional consultant, Brenda McDonald, at Dorrance Publishing Company, who first read my manuscript and stated that she loved it. Thank you, Samantha DeFlitch, my writing coach who patiently and thoroughly proofread my manuscript and made much needed suggestions. Finally, I thank Dorrance Publishing Company for accepting my manuscript for publication. To God be the glory!

1

Growing Up in Sweet Home Alabama

There was a time when home, church, and school worked in unison together. The people respected each other's home, they respected the church, and they respected the school. It was the responsibility of the parents to nurture, raise, and teach the children right from wrong. It was the responsibility of the church to accept each person as she/he was and teach everyone God's principles and promises, and it was the responsibility of the school to provide comprehensive quality education to all children. The home, church, and school were the village and the village was only as strong as its weakest link. This was the era I was born into.

I was raised in a spiritual home by my devoted Methodist parents. I was baptized as a newborn, and I grew up knowing that God had blessed me in the presence of my pastor, parents, relatives, and members of my church, which was Saint Stephens African Methodist Episcopal (A.M.E) Church in Columbia, Alabama. Saint Stephens A.M.E. church was a rural church located on Alabama highway 95. It took Daddy approximately 15 minutes to drive from home to Saint Stephens. Sunday School was held every Sunday and worship services were held two Sundays of each month. On the Sundays that my home church did not have worship services, we attended other churches' worship services. It did not matter whether they were Methodist, Baptist, or Pentecostal, as long as Jesus Christ was the head of each church.

My mother and father read the Bible to my siblings and me frequently as we gathered around the fireplace in the evenings. I am the seventh child of 18 children. My baptism was confirmed at a very young age. I was taught the Lord's Prayer and several Bible verses before I learned to read. I heard numerous Biblical stories told by Daddy and in Sunday School. I knew several of them from memory at a very young age. Daddy was a gifted storyteller, and I was mesmerized by the different tones expressed in his voice and the skillful way he emphasized certain words.

Sometimes as we gathered around the fireplace, Mama and Daddy focused on teaching us proper deportment that was suitable for my siblings and me. My parents emphasized to all of us that our behaviors in public represented the entire Williams family and that we were being raised to be upright and contributing individuals. In addition, those family gatherings were opportunities for all of to share with Mama and Daddy the things and events that were going on in our lives.

Mama was a gentle woman with a soft voice. She would go about doing her housework, raising and nurturing us as she sang some of her favorite spiritual songs. When Mama was not singing, she would hum the songs. I thought Mama had a gifted voice. Even today, I still believe this. I am still amazed how Mama completed the endless tasks of housework and raising and nurturing 18 children every day without losing her mind. All 18 of us were only a little over a year apart in age. I honestly believe that since Mama was an only child, she felt that being the mother of 18 children was a blessing rather than a curse.

Not only was Mama an only child, but I was told that Mama's youngest cousin was ten years older than her. Although being an only child had many advantages, I can only imagine that Mama was very lonely at times during her childhood, especially during rainy days, when she was not permitted to venture outside to play with her friends. Back in the day, children were encouraged to play outside and move around on a daily basis, and this was the same way Mama taught me. When Daddy went to work, Mama was inside nursing her babies and during housework and the other children were outside playing. I only came inside to eat, drink, bathe, and sleep during my formative years.

I was never lonely during my formative years because I had plenty of sisters and brothers. My siblings and I enjoyed playing dodge ball in the front yard. Mama and Daddy would be at each end throwing the ball occasionally. But most of the time, this task was accomplished by two of my older siblings. The purpose was to hit one of us with the ball to get us out of the game. Usually, the youngest ones were thrown out first. I remember being thrown out very early in those games. Another game my siblings and I played together was racing. I remember racing down the hill, which was located near Macedonia Baptist Church and ended directly in front of my parents' house. And there was a hill in the opposite direction that was located a short distance from my first cousins' house and ended near a bridge. On some occasions, Mama and Daddy raced down these hills with my siblings and me. My siblings and I played these two games year round, and I grew up enjoying playing and walking in the rain and in the cold.

Mama had a weekly washday, which depended on the weather. On her washday, the oldest child had to take care of the younger children while Mama was washing the clothes. Washing clothes took the entire day because everything was done by hand. Daddy would build a fire under the large boiling pot to heat up the water to be used. Then Daddy would fill up the large tin tubs with water from the well and add hot water from the boiling pot. Mama would separate the dirty clothes and proceed to wash the lighter colored clothes first, beginning with the white ones. She used a scrub board for the dirtiest clothes. There were two or three tubs of water used for rinsing the clothes. After rinsing each load of clothes, Mama would hang them on clotheslines outside for drying.

Occasionally, Mama would stop washing and come in the house to check on her children. I remember having to watch my younger siblings on washdays while I was still too young to attend school. During my formative years, the school district did not have any preschool and kindergarten programs for African Americans in Alabama.

On this particular washday, I fell asleep while my younger siblings were in my care. My brother, David, had crawled into the fireplace and burned his forehead. Mama came in and discovered David lying in the fireplace in the hot ashes. Mama's hysterical screaming woke me and then I realized what had happened. Eventually, Daddy appeared, summed up the situation, and he and Mama quickly took David to the nearest hospital, which was 18 miles away.

When they returned home from the hospital, neither one of them scolded me. They both knew that it was an unfortunate accident and nothing could change what had happened. My tears and body language told them how terrible I felt. I learned a valuable lesson that day: I would never fall asleep ever again when I was in charge of taking care of my younger siblings.

Since there was no official preschool or kindergarten programs for African Americans in Alabama, all children who would be entering first grade the next school year attended school with their older siblings for a couple weeks or months before the current school year ended. This allowed the entering first graders to become familiar with what would be required of them in first grade. I clearly remember when my older sisters, Arola and Carrie, took me to school with them. Although I do not recall the details of those days I spent in school with them, I remember how excited I was riding the school bus and seeing all of the other students and teachers. I was eagerly looking forward to starting school in the first grade.

The name of the school was Columbia High, and all grades were located on the same campus. The Town of Columbia had two separate schools systems – one for black and brown students and one for white students. It turned out that attending school was my favorite activity from first grade and beyond. I enjoyed riding the bus each day and learning new things. I looked forward to Monday mornings and dreaded Friday afternoons. All subject matters were my favorite subjects – I couldn't pick just one favorite. I excelled in reading, writing, arithmetic, social studies, history, geography, science, and gym. Fall and winter became my favorite seasons because I was in school five days each week, doing what I enjoyed the most: learning.

My first-grade teacher was very smart and firm but also kind and demonstrated her love for teaching.

Whenever I mastered a lesson in any subject, she would praise me and say, "Margaret, I knew you could do it." Those wide smiles and verbal praises made me feel good internally and motivated me to work harder. I believe her name was Mrs. Robinson. She was very tall and slender and wore beautiful dress suits. She had beautiful straight white teeth, and whenever she smiled, her entire face lit up.

I adjusted very well to first grade. I obeyed my teacher's instructions. I learned to raise my hand whenever I needed her attention, to participate in class, or needed her permission to go to the bathroom. Many of my classmates didn't adjust well. Now, Mrs. Robinson took her job as an educator very seriously. She did not waste her time and was determined that students did not waste theirs. Because I had two older sisters, I could verbally say my alphabets and numbers at least up to ten. Mrs. Robinson would have each student practice writing the alphabets and numbers on the blackboard first because as we made mistakes, they could easily be erased. I clearly remember struggling as I learned to write. Verbally saying my alphabets and numbers were much easier for me than learning to write them. Mrs. Robinson always scheduled story time for her first graders, and I enjoyed all of her stories. My parents could not afford to buy children books for us to learn to read at home.

In the evenings and weekends, Cassie and I played school. I was always the teacher and Cassie was always the student. I imitated Mrs. Robinson during each class session. Everything I learned in school, I taught Cassie. By the time Cassie was in the first grade, she knew as much as I had learned during my entire first-grade. Mrs. Robinson commented to some of the other teachers that Cassie was much smarter than her other students. Cassie and I continued this practice throughout our formal educational experiences at Columbia High School. Cassie and I were more than sisters from the onset. I was never jealous of her, and she was never jealous of me. Since I was only one year older than Cassie and we were both girls, we had much in common. I had four older brothers and two older sisters. I discovered that my brothers mostly complained that I was a nuisance to them, and they never played school with me or helped me with my schoolwork.

The scheduled recesses were always fun because my classmates and I could run around playing tag games as we dirtied up our clothes. Mrs. Robinson would supervise every recess as she talked with some of the other teachers.

My classmates and I were always under the watchful eyes and care of our teachers. And as a result, we grew up feeling safe and secure at all times.

Back in the day, all of the parents knew each other in my hometown, which meant they associated with each other in their homes, churches, schools, ball games, and fish fry parties on Saturday nights. The teachers were well respected among the parents; they were close friends with many parents, who expected the teachers to educate their children. So, the parents and teachers worked collaboratively for the welfare of all children and for the benefit of the community-at-large.

Because all of the parents knew each other, they were the eyes and ears for the community-at-large. All parents relied on each other to model proper behaviors in the presence of children. I remember that my parents did not initially have a telephone, and yet by the time I would arrive home from school, they already knew everything that happened that day. The parents embraced the African proverb that says it takes a village to raise a child.

The philosophy of the parents and teachers coincided. My parents were kind and loving, but they were disciplinarians, too. All of the teachers were the same.

At home, whenever I was disobedient, I was verbally disciplined. By the time I was in the first-grade, and depending on the seriousness of my disobedience, I would receive either verbal scolding and have to stand in a corner, or the teacher would hit me in the palm of my hand with a ruler. These types of corporal disciplines were permitted beginning in the first-grade, and my parents disciplined me the same way.

My older siblings called me Miss Goodie Two Shoes, because I very rarely disobeyed and would encourage my younger siblings to do the same. I am not saying that I was a saint. But too frequently, I had seen Mama and Daddy discipline my older siblings. I learned very early what I could get away with and what I could not. So, I tried my best to avoid all kinds of corporal punishment.

Mama and Daddy used a type of corporal punishment called whipping. When my siblings and I were going to be whipped, we were sent to the backyard to select our own switch (tree branch). If we did not bring back the correct size switch, we were sent to the backyard again. None of us wanted to select too big of a switch, and we knew the switch had be flexible. If the switch had too many leaves, Mama and Daddy would remove them.

Every time I was going to be whipped by either Mama or Daddy, I immediately began to cry. As I proceeded to the backyard to select my switch, I cried louder. As I returned with a switch, I was screaming loudly, dancing and moving around before the first lick contacted my legs. Mama's whippings were very brief with few words. But Daddy would give us a long lecture first; he expected us to promise him that we would not disobey again and then a whipping proceeded. Of course, history always repeated itself.

Hot and humid weather in Alabama began very early each year and lasted late in each year. It seemed to me that I endured at least six months of very hot and humid weather each year. At the age of six, my older siblings and I were determined to build a swimming pool in our front yard. Every day after Daddy left home, we would begin digging a hole in the front yard, and every evening when Daddy returned home, we had to fill in the hole.

One day I was sitting on a wagon with my baby sibling in my arms, and I fell into the hole that all of us had dug that day. When Mama heard me scream loudly, she ran from inside the house, took my baby sibling from my arms, and sent one of my older siblings to notify Daddy. I had managed to hold onto my baby sibling as my back made contact with the ground. As a result, my back had taken the brunt of the fall. My baby sibling was crying loudly and constantly from fright. There was no way Mama or Daddy could be sure that the baby had not been hurt. Since I was only six-years-old, I would not have been able to convince them. Daddy arrived home and quickly drove Mama and my baby sibling to the hospital, which was 18 miles away. I, on the other hand, was left to nurse my own bruises. The emergency room physician told Mama and Daddy that my baby sibling had only been frightened from the fall.

When Mama and Daddy returned home from the hospital, they did not scold me verbally or whip me. However, Daddy promised all of us that if he discovered any holes in the front yard in the future that none of us would be able to sit down for months or even years. My siblings and I never dug any more holes. Mama and Daddy never took to me to a doctor to have my back examined. I suffered back problems from that day forward, but I never told my parents because I felt guilty about disobeying Daddy and that I had gotten what I deserved.

I adored Daddy so much that at the age of seven, I asked permission to accompany him to work after lunch. When we arrived at Daddy's destination, I was surprised to discover that it was a cotton field. I did not want to believe what I was seeing. Multiple thoughts raced through my mind all at once. I remembered that Daddy and my older siblings were talking and laughing as they approached our house at noon and in the evening many times. I thought that all of them had been enjoying themselves on those trips away from home, and this was the primary reason I wanted to accompany Daddy after lunch on that fateful day. I felt helpless and doomed, and the worst thing was that I was responsible for my dismal situation.

Unfortunately for me, my carefree days ended abruptly that afternoon as I began to face the stark realities of how difficult my life would be from then onward. Daddy gave me a cotton sack to put around my neck and onto my shoulder. He chose three rows of cotton: two for him and one for me. I watched Daddy as he picked cotton and began to imitate him to the best of my ability. Picking cotton was very painful to the fingers and back. The sun was so hot that I felt as if I were going to burn up and die.

That particular afternoon was the most horrific experience I had ever endured in my seven years of life. I could not drink enough water to clench my thirst. My fingers ached so bad that I felt they were not my own fingers anymore, and my back felt that it would break any second from the excruciating pain. Finally, it was time to go home. After all of the sacks of cotton were weighed and emptied, Daddy, my older siblings and I walked home. Maybe Daddy and my older siblings were talking and laughing among themselves as we walked home; I am definitely sure that I did neither.

As soon as I had the opportunity, I warned Cassie and Paul to never ask Daddy's permission to accompany him anywhere because if they did, they would end up picking cotton in the hot sun just as I had done. Cassie and Paul never asked Daddy's permission to accompany him during that week and I was relieved.

The next morning, Daddy woke me up and told me it was time to go the cotton field.

I quickly said, "Daddy, I don't want to go!"

Daddy responded, "Baby, you did such a good job yesterday, and you have to go to work now." I quickly went to Arola, my oldest sister, and asked her to tell Daddy to let me stay home. She said she couldn't do that because she had to go to the cotton fields herself.

Arola said, "Once we start working in the fields, we have no other choice." Henceforth, fall and winter became my favorite seasons because there was no field work for me to perform during these two seasons of each year.

After having to work in the cotton fields all week, I began to look forward to attending church every Sunday. It was a time that I could be with my friends. We all attended school together and many of us worked in the fields together. For me, attending church was all about being with my siblings and friends. During my childhood, the majority of the parents had large families, and the number of children attending Sunday School and worship services far exceeded the number of adults. For example, if there were 50 adults attending church on a regular basis and each family had an average of five children, then there would be well over 100 children in church. Even if there were less than 50 adults attending church on a regular basis, the number of children attending church far exceeded the number of adults on any given Sunday.

Daddy would take all of the children to Sunday School first who were old enough to go to the bathroom by ourselves and/or tell someone we needed to go. Then he would make a second trip to pick up Mama and the younger children after Sunday School ended. He was the Superintendent of Sunday School and a deacon (steward) in the church. I was very happy when I became old enough to attend Sunday School every Sunday. Besides,

I knew Monday followed Sunday. Then I would have five horrible days of working in the fields during the summer months.

Starting at age seven, I missed attending school the entire month of September each year to help pick cotton. Then, on my first day of school, I didn't have all of the required textbooks because the state of Alabama required the parents to purchase all textbooks for their children. I was unsure whether this applied to the white parents. Not having all of my textbooks presented many challenges for me each school day. My teachers wrote much of my homework assignments on the blackboard, and I had to copy this information down on paper. If I made any mistakes when I copied this information, it meant that my responses would be incorrect. I learned to double check everything I copied thoroughly to prevent me from getting the answers wrong.

My parents were grateful that they could provide me with four complete outfits to wear to school, which included my church clothes and at least two pairs of shoes that fit. At this age, I was not concerned with clothes and shoes as long as I had something to wear.

Usually by the age of seven, all of the children were permitted to eat at the dining room table with the rest of the family. The younger children continued to eat all of their meals on a pallet on the kitchen floor. The younger children were always served first. For me, this was the only disadvantage of eating at the dining table along with the rest of the family. Thankfully, the younger children sitting at the table were served before the older children and the parents. I don't remember if our meals were chaotic, but all of them were very noisy as we eagerly looked forward to being served. Mama and Daddy would remind all of us to stop talking when our mouths were full and to keep our elbows off the table. Usually, it turned out that my siblings and I did not obey our parents very well because we kept eating and talking simultaneously. Eventually, my siblings and I recognized our parents' stern facial expressions of their displeasure with our table etiquette. Gradually, my parents were pleased with our table manners.

Mama would wake up very early in the mornings before the sun came up and cook breakfast, which usually consisted of biscuits, eggs, bacon, and grits. Mama's biscuits were always delicious and tasted best when eaten hot with melted butter. Lunch and dinner had similar foods. We never ate sandwiches for lunch. Mama could make the best fried chicken and sweet or white potatoes were eaten daily for lunch and dinner, although the meat and vegetables varied. My parents raised chicken and hogs, and feeding them became the responsibilities of the younger children each day. At the time, I thought this task was very difficult to accomplish each day. I don't remember how often I had to feed these animals daily. But this was actually the main reason I had asked Daddy if I could accompany him after lunch on that particular day. I hated feeding the chicken and hogs so much that I thought I would have more fun accompanying Daddy.

The summer I was turned eight, I was taught how to hoe cotton and peanuts, to pick butter beans and peas, and to pull weeds from the growing cotton and peanut plants. Some of the weeds were taller than I was. Usually Daddy and my brother, Jacob, would come to my rescue. Both of them helped and watched over me as I struggled to perform the task at hand and keep up the pace. I dreaded every summer and eagerly looked forward to every fall. As summer ended each year, I knew the first Monday in October would be approaching in about two weeks. This meant no more fieldwork for me until May of the next year.

October heralded both the end of fieldwork and the coming of Halloween. Maybe some families decorated for

Halloween, but Halloween was never a big deal for my siblings and me. Mama and Daddy never bought extra candy for us, they never bought Halloween outfits for us, and they never decorated the yard signifying Halloween. And I never felt that I missed out of any Halloween celebrations.

Now, Christmas was a different story altogether. I would make my Christmas wish list every year, and I never received what I wished for. It was a constant disappointment that I endured every Christmas morning. I did not understand why Santa did not bring me the presents I had wished for. Jacob told me that Daddy was Santa, and Daddy could not afford to buy specific presents for each of us.

This was how I discovered that Mama and Daddy could not afford to be extravagant at Christmas or any other time. Usually for Christmas, the age specific toys were shared among the younger children and the other toys that were not age specific were shared among the older ones. I remember for one Christmas, Daddy had assembled a gym set and bicycle to be shared by all of us. When my brothers weren't home, Cassie and I taught each other how to ride the bicycle. But when they were home, we never went near that bike. If Mama and Daddy managed to buy dolls for any of the girls, we shared them with each other.

All of us learned the principle of sharing at a very young age, whether we liked it or not. I never remember receiving any presents for my birthdays, although Mama, Daddy, and my siblings always wished me a happy birthday each year. It made my birthday very special to me by remembering that my birthday was all mine, and it was the day God gave me as a perfect gift to my parents. So, I used my imagination to feel very special to God and myself. Because I am the only one of the 18 children born in the month of July, I did not have to share the entire month with anyone in my family. July was my birth month all to myself. Knowing this fact caused me to feel even better.

At the age of nine, I began not to look forward to Saturdays. My two older sisters, Arola and Carrie, left home when I was nine-years-old. I clearly remember the day my childhood changed, as if it were yesterday. It was the day when Mama called to me to come in and help her in the kitchen. I was busy playing hopscotch in the front yard with my siblings when Mama called to me. On that day, I lost the remaining free time to be a little girl.

Mama told me that I needed to help her with preparing the meals from then on. I was too short to reach the pots on the stove, so Mama had me kneel in a chair each time I needed to stir the foods in the different pots. It became routine that Mama would prepare all the foods, and I watched and stirred the foods as they simmered. Then I turned off the oven and burners once all the foods were ready.

During that same summer, I remember shelling and snapping peas for canning along with some of my siblings when there weren't any field work left to perform. Canning was one of those major family affair jobs that had to be done every summer. I was not permitted to use sharp knives, so Mama and some of my older siblings peeled and cut up all of the fruits and vegetables. Shelling and snapping peas were boring and tiresome. But when winter came, the canned vegetables and fruits were blessings for all of us every day at breakfast, lunch, and dinner because we ate well and our stomachs were full. Then I would be very grateful that Mama, Daddy, my siblings and I had performed those boring and tiresome chores during the previous summer.

Because my two older sisters had left home soon after graduating from high school and I had inherited the chores they had previously performed, I was even more excited about attending school in the fourth-grade that year. However, I would have the toughest elementary teacher in the entire school. Her name was Mrs. Codman, and my older siblings had warned me about her. They emphasized the fact that I must behave appropriately at all times and do my best because Mrs. Codman did not take any mess. As it turned out, Mrs. Codman was no different than all of my previous teachers to me. I just followed her instructions about everything, made sure I turned in all of my assignments on time, and readily participated in class discussions.

The summer I turned ten was the same as the previous one. The only happy thought that I remember from that summer was that I would have Mrs. McLoyd as my teacher. She had the reputation of being the kindest, gentlest, friendliest, and most approachable teacher at the school. I was not concerned about any of her attributes because we had been her neighbors for years. Mrs. McLoyd already knew my family very well.

In addition to all of her teaching responsibilities, Mrs. McLoyd was responsible for preparing us for pre-adolescent and adolescent facts of life. At the age of ten, I was not thinking about any changes my body would undergo, and the film that Mrs. McLoyd had chosen to generate discussions was more embarrassing than helpful at the time. I believed my classmates felt the same way because we had very few questions to ask after the movie ended. And comparing my current body to what had been shown in that movie was beyond my comprehension since my body was slim and flat all over.

Up to this point, I actually thought a special stork brought Mama a new baby every time I had a new sibling. And besides, what I had seen and heard as I watched the movie was so foreign to me that I could not wrap my brain around it. I decided that I would not concern myself right then, because if this would happen, it would be far into my future.

By the time I was 12-years-old, I had done much thinking about my current life and my future life. For one thing, I knew I did not want my adult life to be anything similar to my current life. Just surviving day to day was a challenge. Daddy had stopped sharecropping the previous fall. As long as we lived on the farm, my family and I had enough foods to eat every day, although milk was scarce sometimes. Some of the meals may not have been well balanced and healthy, but at least our stomachs were always full. After Daddy stopped farming, there were many days when the only thing for breakfast was sugar mixed with water and a little vanilla flavor and biscuits.

Even when Daddy was sharecropping, there were many days we did not have milk to drink since we only had one cow. A large family such as mine needed two or more milking cows. But now milk became almost non-existent because my parents did not own the one milking cow anymore.

When I was in the seventh-grade, I had developed the habit of spending every lunch period in the school library reading magazines and books. Reading was my favorite past time. But the primary reason I went to the library every day at lunchtime was because I had nothing to eat for lunch. When the bell rang, notifying me that it was time to return to class, I would stop by the water fountain and drink lots of water to make my stomach feel full.

One day, Mrs. Hines, the school librarian, said to me that she noticed that I spent every lunch period reading books in the library. She asked me if I would object if she recommended books for me to read. I replied by saying no and thanked her. Out of respect, I did not have the nerve to refuse Mrs. Hines, and she proceeded to give me a list of books to check out of the library. Mrs. Hines requested that I give her an oral report about each book. Therefore, each time I finished a book, I gave Mrs. Hines an oral report. After a short period of time, Mrs. Hines suggested that I give her a written report. By this time, I was very excited about every book I read and eagerly did what she requested without delay. Mrs. Hines observed the change in me, and I could tell by her body language that she enjoyed our sessions together.

Mrs. Hines was also my English teacher. She recommended me to perform a monologue play for the school in the evening on a Friday night. She said that I had the gift of acting because she had observed my body language, facial expressions, changes in my voices, and the dramatic way I used my hands as I gave her a verbal summary of each book I had finished reading. Mrs. Hines said that I became the heroine in each book, and I would perform very well in this play in front of an audience. I agreed, and Mrs. Hines began to coach me after school.

Mrs. Hines sent word home by all of my classmates about the upcoming play. She also requested all of the teachers to do the same. The play would be a fundraiser for the school. I do not remember the details. However,

I do remember that I did not receive any money for my performance, and it never occurred to me to ask or expect any payment.

On the day of the play, I was very nervous and I told Mrs. Hines this. She could tell that I was very nervous from my body language and voice. I practiced slow, deep breathing and completed my last rehearsal. Mrs. Hines was the mistress of ceremony on opening night and she introduced me. I was so nervous and did not pay attention to her opening introduction. I was instructed to already be in place on the stage when the curtains opened. As the curtains opened, there was loud applause. I forgot about my nerves and went into character. I received a standing ovation. Afterward, everyone told me that my performance was outstanding. Each year afterwards, I was chosen to perform in at least two school plays. I even contemplated going to Hollywood and becoming a professional actress one day.

Reading gave my life a new dimension and meaning. I was the heroine in each book. I traveled all over the world; I was enjoying life and finding new adventures. I was very happy and successful during my reading. Through my reading, I discovered that many black folks had been very successful in Massachusetts. They even had attended colleges and universities such as Tufts and Harvard. I was very impressed with this information. My outlook completely changed all because of the different books I was reading. I had always been serious about school and learning, but now it was with more passion, dedication, and commitment.

Even Mama noticed that I did not complain as much about all of the house chores, cooking, and taking care of my younger siblings. I became more patient, kind, and gentle with my younger siblings. Shampooing and conditioning their hair were not burdens anymore. I smiled and laughed more, and I developed the habit of being more positive and less negative. I learned to keep my mouth shut if I did not have anything good or positive to say. I learned to actively listen, to reject what was false, and to think for myself. I learned to become more obedient to my parents and more considerate of other people's feelings. I kept my deep and personal feelings about different things to myself. I was beginning to discover that my desires for my future were not as important to anyone but me.

My eighth-grade school year was uneventful, except that I got my period that year. I was actually 13-and-nine-months-old when I got my period. My fifth-grade teacher had shown a movie about menstruation, which included the hygiene supplies I would need and proper hygiene instructions. So, I was aware of the changes my body would undergo. I just did not know when. When it did finally happen, it was early one morning as I was dressing for school. I rushed and told Mama. Mama went and opened a drawer in her bedroom and removed folded pieces of cloth and handed them to me. She patiently explained what I was supposed to do with these cloths. The problem was that Mama's instructions conflicted with what I had learned in the fifth-grade. I was very confused, and therefore, I rejected Mama's instructions. I never considered that my rejection had hurt her feelings. I quickly finished dressing and walked past my school to Daddy's job for his help.

I asked the owner of the fertilizer plant permission to see my daddy. Daddy came outside, and I told him that I had become a woman that morning. He wanted to know if I had told Mama and I said yes, but I did not understand what Mama wanted me to do. Daddy told me to go to Bristow's Store, purchase everything I needed, and charge it to his account. He told me to do this every month.

As the months passed, I became aware that my parents did not earn much money, and therefore, many material things I desired were beyond what they could afford. I also became aware that the majority of black folks were not much better off than we were, but most white folks were. I became embarrassed about the house I lived in, about my clothes, about my shoes, and winter coat. There was only one other family with more children than my parents had. In the eighth-grade, I became a very close friend with one of the girls from this large family. Her name was Irma. Although we were both in the eighth grade, Irma was a year older than I was. Irma did not have many clothes either, although the house she and her family lived in was in much better condition than my house. My house was unpainted, but her house was painted. In addition, her house had a screen door and a strong front door. My house only had a front door held shut from the inside with a piece of rectangular-shaped wood that was called a latch.

One day after school, I was very excited about this little rhyming song Irma had taught me during our recess. It went like this: *I'm a red-hot mama from a red-hot town. It takes a red-hot daddy to cool me down.* I even sang the rhyme to Mama. Mama was shocked to hear me sing this rhyme to her. My eldest brother, Jacob, heard what I said and quickly and severely reprimanded me and told me to never sing or say this rhyme again. He said it was a nasty and distasteful rhyme and good girls didn't sing or say such things. In the eighth-grade, I was 13-years-old. I had no idea that the rhyme Irma had taught me was nasty or distasteful. Actually, I was confused. I never said or sang that rhyme aloud to anyone again. I went to school the next day and told Irma that I had gotten in trouble with Mama and Jacob when I had sang the rhyme. I never learned any more rhymes from Irma, and I did not understand the meaning of that rhyme until several years later.

Later that same school year, Irma quit school. Then we only saw each other when I visited her church. The next year, Irma married one of the school bus drivers. I did not understand why Irma would quit school, and she never explained to me why. She got married at age 15. Her reasoning for marrying was beyond my comprehension.

Age 14 was a crucial time for me. I was unsatisfied with the conditions of my life. The summer I was turning 14, my sister, Carrie, needed a babysitter for her three children, Michael, Felecia, and Alan. Babysitting three children may seem to some as an awesome task, but to me, it was a godsend. It was a blessing for me sent by God through Carrie. I was thrilled. I thought to myself, *if Mama and Daddy said yes to Carrie's request, I wouldn't have to do any kind of fieldwork until the beginning of September.* This meant that as soon as the current school year ended, I would ride the Greyhound bus to Dothan, Alabama, which was 18 miles away. Carrie lived in Dothan and the school year would end the latter part of May. Then I would have all of June, July, and August to babysit my two nephews and one niece. Thank God!

Carrie was married to Mack. They lived in a government apartment. At the time, I did not know all of these apartments were known as projects or government apartments. All I knew was that all of them were much better looking than my house and those I had lived in all my life. Carrie's apartment had running water in the kitchen and bathroom. All of the floors were tiled. The front and back yards were covered with green grass and someone kept the grass cut on a regular basis. It was years before I learned that Carrie and Mack had lived in the projects, which were classified as low-income apartments. To me at the time, I thought they were living their dreams.

Babysitting my nephews and niece was not hard work at all. Besides, Carrie and Mack's apartment had air conditioning. I had nothing to complain about. Carrie cooked the meals every day, and when the children slept, I cleaned the apartment. I was very good at cleaning and washing clothes. Carrie had a washer and all I had to do was to hang the wet clothes, sheets, and towels on the outside clotheslines to dry. Then, later, I would remove them from the clotheslines, fold them, and iron the rest. That was the best summer I had ever experienced during my entire teenage years.

But not everything was great about that summer. I wanted to wear beautiful summer outfits like the white girls. I yearned to be able to walk to the drug store and purchase a cone of ice cream, and I wanted to learn to swim and go swimming in the local pool during those hot and humid summer days. But none of those things were available to me. My four older brothers learned to swim in creeks in the woods. I was not allowed to accompany them. They told me that there were all kinds of snakes in the water. After that I never asked or wanted to go with them, although my desire to learn to swim remained.

By the time I was 14-years-old, I had been working in the fields for seven long hot and humid summers.

Early one morning in September, as I waited for the driver to pick up my siblings and me to take us to the cotton field, I stood in my parents' backyard and prayed fervently to God about my dismal situation. I cried out to God that morning with tears in my eyes and a heavy heart. I felt burdened. I asked God if this was all I had to look forward to. I don't recall how long I prayed that morning, but when I finished, my heart was not heavy anymore. I sensed that God had something better and wonderful for me in the future. Although the conditions of my life remained the same, I came to realize that this was my parents' life. Because I was a minor and under their care, it was a life I had to live until I was old enough to leave home when I turned 18 or graduated from high school. I decided that I was going to become a doctor. And I would figure out the type of doctor later.

I developed a crush on a boy named Wallace when I was 14. He lived a few doors down the hill from me and on the same street. I thought he was the cutest boy and the best dressed one. When I was 15, Mama and Daddy permitted him to come to my house to court me. He and I, along with my family, would sit in the living room watching television together. At 9:00 PM, Wallace would have to leave. My parents did not permit courting after 9:00 PM. Daddy noticed that Wallace was a frequent visitor to our house and that he had bought me a watch with a matching bracelet.

One day, Daddy said to me that if I fell in love with Wallace, we would get married and start a family. He continued telling me that in order to earn enough money to live on, Wallace would have me working in the fields picking cotton because Wallace had dropped out of school and did not have any vocational skills of any kind. I attempted to tell Daddy that I was not interested in marrying Wallace now or in the future because I wanted to attend college and then medical school.

Daddy said, "Baby, when you are truly in love, the only thing you want to do is marry the one you truly love." He advised me to only accept dates from boys or men who I felt would make good husbands in the future. Daddy abruptly ended our conversation and went about his business. He left me with many things to think about.

I was left pondering what Daddy had said to me. I told myself that there was no way I would be picking cotton or doing any other type of fieldwork when I was grown. Immediately, I made up my mind what I had to do. The next day, I returned the watch and bracelet to Wallace and told him that I did not like him anymore. I did not give him any explanations. As a matter of fact, I avoided looking in his direction ever again, and I never smiled back at him when I caught him staring in my direction or talked to him anymore. I had decided that nothing was going to prevent me from attending college and medical school.

Every time I thought of picking cotton as an adult was enough for me to stay focused and not become involved with boys. I enjoyed attending dances and socializing with boys, but that was all. I decided that I would not have a boyfriend because having a boyfriend would lead to falling in love, getting married, and working in the cotton field if I remained in Alabama after graduating from high school. I began to realize that just thinking about what I wanted my future to look like was not going to work for me. I had to begin making concrete plans. But, at that time, I did not know where to turn except to my church and school.

As a teenager, I was very active in my church youth's ministries. I attended Sunday School on a regular basis, I sang in the youths' choir, and I was a youth usher. I was in good standing in the church. But then I committed my first theft outside of my home at age 14. I had often taken fried chicken breasts without permission at home. Being one of 18 children, there was no guarantee that I would be given a piece of the chicken breast since it was the only piece I liked. So, as often as possible, I had taken the fried chicken breast without Mama's permission. Each time I reasoned that it was worth the scolding from Mama. After spending three full months in Dothan, Alabama, I had returned home. It was now the month of September. My first public crime occurred on a day that I was scheduled to attend an evening revival. On this particular day, I was scheduled to usher at one of the local churches in my hometown, which was Mount Olive Baptist Church (MOBC).

Daddy had given me permission to quit working in the field at 3:00 PM, so that I could go home, bathe, and dress. Then I would have ample time to walk to the MOBC, receive my instructions from the adult usher in charge, and be ready to perform my duties at the appropriate time. Although I had eaten lunch, I was famished and my stomach was letting me know it. As I was walking to MOBC, I stopped and went inside Bristow's Grocery Store and stole two packs of Hostess chocolate covered cupcakes. Those cupcakes were the best cupcakes I had ever eaten.

I arrived at MOBC as planned, met with the adult usher in charge, and I was in place, ready to greet the first person entering the front door with a wide smile on my face. During the sermon, I felt as if the guest preacher was staring directly at me as he preached. I felt that the minister knew that I had stolen those cupcakes, and through his sermon, he was admonishing me. I began to feel very guilty about my theft and wanted to cry. Up until this point, I had not experienced any guilt. I had only experienced the great satisfaction of not being hungry anymore.

By the time I arrived home later that night, I was crying uncontrollably and felt awful. I confessed my transgression to Daddy as I cried and explained everything, starting from being very hungry as I left home, stopping in Bristow's Grocery Store, stealing two packs of cupcakes, and thoroughly enjoying every bite. I confessed to Daddy that at the time, those cupcakes were the best tasting cupcakes I had ever eaten and that I had felt not an ounce of guilt until the minister began to preach. Then suddenly, I was overwhelmed with guilt and shame. It took all of my concentration and strength to keep from having an emotional crisis while I was ushering. After I stopped talking, I continued crying, and so Daddy took me in his arms and comforted me by saying he could tell I that was remorseful about my transgression. He said besides, God had already forgiven me. So, now forgive yourself. In a matter of a few minutes, I stopped crying and began to feel much better. Daddy's words continued to resonate with me the rest of the night, and I was able to sleep with a guilt-free conscious.

The next day, I went back to cotton field as if I had never stolen anything other than pieces of Mama's fried chicken breasts. Since I had forgiven myself, I went about my assigned chores as usual. I stayed out of trouble and followed my parents' rules without questioning their authority. Yet my sister, Cassie, and I had numerous conversations about our dismal situations and how we were disgusted with everything. Mama and Daddy were the main subjects of our private conversations, although there were many other things we opposed. We made plans that we would leave home as soon as possible, and soon as possible was just not soon enough for us.

By the way, Cassie and I had run away from home together six years earlier. We were still living on a farm then, and Cassie and I were tired of picking cotton and doing all the other farm chores. So, we each tied a few clothes in tablecloth and left home. We had taken water and food with us. Every time we heard a car pass, we would hide, and if someone was sitting on their porch or standing in their yard, we would cross to the other side of the road and act as if we did not see them.

As the day passed, the sun eventually went down. We began to hear strange noises, which frightened us so badly that we could not return home quickly enough. By the time we arrived back home, it was dinnertime and everyone was eating their dinner. Cassie and I sat down at the table and began eating, too. Mama and Daddy never asked us why we were late coming to the table or where we had been. Their behaviors remained a mystery to us. Cassie and I decided soon afterwards that we would wait until we were much older to permanently leave home for good.

I was very athletic and tried out for the girls' basketball team in the ninth-grade. Daddy encouraged me to participate in sports. My school did not have a gymnasium and all of our basketball practices and games were held outside. This was the normal situation for all of the school's black and brown students attended in Alabama, at least in the part of Alabama I lived in. None of the schools my school played against had indoor gymnasiums either. My school's logo was Gators. My position on the basketball team was as a guard. I played hard and physical, and I practiced just as hard and physical. The basketball coach, Mr. Bynum, coached both the girls' and boys' basketball teams. My school did not have a separate junior and varsity teams because there were not enough students. The only drawback to playing girls' basketball was the fact that the teams had to leave school before school ended, and I would miss the remaining classes on those days.

I enjoyed sweating and running. So, I joined the track team in the spring during my first year of high school. Mr. Bynum was the coach of the track team, too, and he did not have an athletic assistant.

The first Friday in May of each year, a local school from Ashford, Alabama and my school held a May Day. This was a day the two schools set aside each year to compete against each other in different athletic events. Every other year, my school would travel to Ashford and compete. Since I was on the track team and was a fast runner, Mr. Bynum prepared me to run the 100 meters and relay races. He would have at least two runners from my school to run the 100 meters race. Sometimes, I would place first, and other times, I placed second. In the relay races, I was either chosen to be the first runner or the last one. Playing sports were excellent outlets for me. Daddy always encouraged me to do my best during each practice session and run my best during each race.

As I maneuvered through high school, my school did not offer any business courses, such as typing and short-hand. But several of my classmates' parents were able to purchase their daughters' typewriters. For the rest of us, we did not have any opportunities to prepare us for any decent jobs after graduating from high school. I had seen many brilliant students who had graduated with high honor, who were valedictorians and salutatorians of their classes, end up working as housekeepers in private homes and as school cafeteria workers.

This prospect of being a housekeeper or cafeteria worker did not appeal to me at all. Most of the guys who graduated from high ended up in low paying jobs, too. I did not want to settle for so little when I knew in my heart that God had something better for me as long as I was willing to work hard for it. For me, working hard meant attending college and medical school. I honestly believed that I would be very happy, very successful, and happily married one day.

Because I was one of 18 children, I was not keen on having any children. And if I did, I would have only one.

I wanted that one to be a girl, so I could buy her all types of beautiful clothes and enroll her in dance and swimming classes. She would take piano and tennis lessons. In other words, if I did have a baby, I would be happily married and my baby girl would have opportunities to everything I never had. I would provide her with dancing and piano lessons, swimming lessons, opportunities to attend summer camp, and all of the other things I missed. But, at this juncture of my life, I doubted that I ever wanted a baby, even if I were happily married.

During the last three years of high school, I discovered that I would never have any practical hands-on experience doing biology laboratory exercises or in all of my other sciences courses because my school science laboratory was ill equipped. It was just an unfinished room without running water, inadequate instruments, supplies, or equipment. I never had opportunities to dissect any animals, such as frogs, salamanders, and pigeons during my high school years because the science laboratory was not equipped for dissecting.

Mr. Thomas taught biology, chemistry, and physics and was an excellent teacher. He would demonstrate each lab exercise. My classmates and I would congregate around him and observe all practical experiments and exercises. Although my school had inadequate science labs, I was a very strong student in the theoretical side of all of the science classes offered at my school and received high grades.

Even though I received high grades and did well in school, I did not know how to apply for college. Daddy had encouraged me to always ask my teachers everything concerning education and college, since he was a fourth-grade scholar. Since I knew Mrs. Hines better than all of my other teachers and I felt very comfortable telling her that I wanted to attend college after graduating from high school. Mrs. Hines said that I needed to take a special exam called SAT. She even looked up the date the next one was scheduled. Mrs. Hines also recommended a book listing colleges and universities, which I could check out from our school library. I was very appreciative for Mrs. Hines's advice and told her how grateful I was. She said that if I needed anything in the future to just ask her. I followed Mrs. Hines's suggestions and took the SAT in my junior year in high school, although I never received the results.

I had the same math teacher from 9th-grade through 12th-grade. Her name was Mrs. Neal. Mathematics was one of my very strong subjects also, and I received high grades from them all. Mrs. Neal taught high school algebra and geometry. My school did not offer any advance level mathematical classes, such as trigonometric and calculus.

I was not concerned about meeting all of my requirements for graduation as some of my classmates were. Since I had never failed any courses during my four years of high school and never had to attend summer school either, I was guaranteed to graduate on time.

Although I was not concerned with graduating on time, I was very concerned about my wardrobe. Having limited clothes to choose from each day, my wardrobe was a serious problem for me. When some of my classmates wanted to dress in certain colors or whatever, I could never do the same. Of course, there were many of us who had limitations with our wardrobes. I remember that one winter during high school that I had to wear my maternal grandmother's winter coat. Everyone knew it had been my grandmother's coat, regardless of all of the alteration it had undergone. I was very embarrassed wearing it every day.

As my senior year was progressing very well academically, the annual Miss Columbia Beauty Pageant held at my school was approaching. Up until my senior year, the majority of the contestants had been primarily students of light-skinned and very few brown of darker skinned. And each year, the winner had been primarily light-skinned. Margret, who was brown-skinned and was one of my classmates, had participated in the Miss Columbia High Beauty Pageant the previous year. To my surprise, Margret won first place in that beauty pageant. Actually, she was the first brown-skinned student I remembered winning the beauty pageant. Margret was crowned Miss Columbia in 1964. Miss Columbia and all of the other winners from the other local schools in Houston County would compete a few weeks later, and the winner and all the contestants who had placed rode on a float during the annual Peanut Festival Parade, which was held in November every year in Dothan, Alabama.

During my senior year in October, I decided to try out for this beauty pageant. Each contestant had to compete in three categories, which were talent, bathing suit, and evening gown. Mrs. Hines was the coach for all contestants. She chose a monologue for me to perform for the talent portion of the pageant. The monologue was based on Simon Peter, as Jesus was being lead to the cross to be crucified. I had several years of acting experience by the time I was in the 12th-grade. Mrs.

Hines dressed me up as a man for my monologue performance, and I disguised my normal voice somewhat. In the role of Simon Peter, I was unrecognizable. I was crowned Miss Columbia of 1965 and became the second brown-skinned student to win this crown in the history of the Columbia High School.

A couple of weeks later, I was to participate in Miss Houston County Beauty Pageant. I did not tell Mrs. Hines that I had borrowed my swimsuit and evening gown from other students for the Miss Columbia pageant. After being crowned Miss Columbia, Mrs. Hines told me that I would need a new bathing suit and gown for the Miss Houston County Pageant. I quickly responded that Daddy would cover the costs of them both. A week before I was scheduled to participate, Mrs. Hines met with Daddy and discovered that he could not afford to buy or contribute to what I needed. All of the teachers contributed money to cover the costs of a new swimsuit and evening gown. Mrs. Hines took me shopping the following day after school. She chose a white swimsuit and pink evening gown.

All of the contestants competing in the Miss Houston County Beauty Pageant had room reservations at the only local black owned hotel in Dothan in advance of the pageant. I am unsure who paid for my hotel stay, but I believe the teachers at my school did. We were all invited to dine with one of the distinguished families in the community. None of us had ever eaten baked apples as it turned out. My tablemates did not exhibit good table etiquette. I, on the other hand, had exhibited excellent table etiquette and proceeded to eat the baked apple. Mrs. Hines was absolutely embarrassed by their conduct and later reprimanded them all.

As the Houston County Beauty Pageant was underway, I performed the same monologue I had previously done. For the swimsuit portion of the pageant, I strutted out in my brand new white swimsuit and matching white high heeled shoes with a wide smile and with an attitude of confidence. My nervousness did not affect my brilliant performance, and I heard people in the audience asking each other which contestant was I since I was unrecognizable to everyone in attendance. I just continued my stride and smiled the entire time as they were attempting to put a face from the talent portion of the competition to the contestant in the white swimsuit.

As I strutted out in my beautiful new evening gown, the people were more in awe of my appearance, attitude of confidence, style, and technique. They were very impressed with my performance and appearance. And even more so when they discovered that I was Miss Columbia, the same contestant who had performed the monologue portraying Simon Peter. They were amazed at the difference in my actual facial appearance. I must admit, I had presented very well. I placed third runner-up that night. As it turned out, I was the first brown-skinned Miss Columbia to have placed as high in the Miss Houston County Beauty Pageant in its entire history.

The newly crowned Miss Houston County had a beautiful decorated queen's float. And all of the runner-up contestants participated in the annual Peanut Festival Parade in the queen's court.

In the 1960s, African Americans were beginning to recognize that beauty came in all shapes, sizes, heights, and colors and no longer accepted the western point of view of beauty. We were black and proud. I was just ahead of many of them. I attributed my knowledge and assurance that I was beautiful to Mama and Daddy. Mama had the most beautiful smooth black skin. I imagined Mama was as beautiful as the Queen of Sheba.

I, on the other hand, suffered with acute cases of acne outbreaks since the age of 12, and I had shared my concerns with Daddy. I was very upset and displeased with the way my face looked. Daddy assured me that my bouts with acne outbreaks were only temporary and recommended that I make sure I cleansed my face thoroughly at least twice a day. Daddy had also told me that God had gifted me with a little intelligence, a little good looks, and a little good figure. Then God had mixed all three characteristics together and made a very smart and beautiful girl with a very good figure named Margaret. I felt good about myself after that, and I embraced what Daddy had told me from then onward.

I was now in the last few months of my senior year in high school, and I was no closer to entering college than I was a year ago. I went to an employment agency in Dothan, Alabama and inquired about a live-in maid job. I told the agency that I was interested in going to Boston as soon as I graduated from high school. That person made all of the arrangements on that same day after inquiring about my graduation date, which was May 27th, 1965. I was scheduled to leave my hometown of Columbia on Sunday, May 31st, 1965 at 12:00 noon.

After arriving home, I told Daddy first about my plans. He tried his best to convince me to change my mind but to no avail. I explained to Daddy that for the last ten years, I had been very afraid of snakes every day as I worked in the fields, and I even had frequent night-mares about them. I said working in the fields from the age of seven had gotten the best of me, and I often wondered if I would be able to endure. Daddy told me that I had been the hardest worker thus far of all of his daughters and the most dependable. On the one hand, I felt good about Daddy's comments. But on the other hand, Daddy's comments did not change my mind.

I apologized to Daddy for not changing my mind and said, "Daddy, I am just too afraid of snakes. Since I will be graduating from high school on Thursday, May 27th, I will be leaving home on Sunday, May 31st." Daddy said, "But you are not 18."

I responded, "I cannot help that I will be graduating from high school before I would be 18." Daddy remained silent after my last remark, and I could tell from his body language that he was saddened.

Then I told Cassie about my plans. Cassie reminded me that we had promised each other years earlier that we would leave home together when we were older. And now I was planning on leaving without her.

Cassie said, "No way I'm staying behind." She went to Dothan to the same employment agency and made similar arrangements. Cassie was 16-years-old and would be entering the 12th-grade in September. I never knew the details of the conversation that Cassie and Daddy had. Cassie never revealed this information to me, and I never asked her about it.

So, at the age of 17, I graduated from high school. Although my GPA was the highest among the senior class, I was denied the honor of being valedictorian. I was told that the reason for this denial was because I had missed too many school days. I was not even considered to be salutatorian. As an alternative, I was chosen alma mater of the graduating class and was one of the three student speakers at commencement. My classmates voted me the one who was most likely to succeed. This news was little consolation to me. I felt that I had been cheated out of the recognition I deserved and that was being valedictorian of my class. It perplexed me that a grown up would be so dishonest and not feel guilty about cheating me out of my hard earned recognition. I wondered if my classmate who was recognized as the valedictorian knew that she had not actually earned it, but it was handed to her by a dishonest teacher.

As my graduation day approached, I put my best efforts forward by hiding my true feelings about the entire scenario surrounding my graduation from high school.

I had made up my mind that I would give the best performance in my life on graduation night. And to make sure, I had devoted several hours rehearsing my presentation. Although I was nervous every time I stood in front of an audience, I had gotten much better hiding it internally. I was determined to out-perform the valedictorian and salutatorian. When my turn came to speak, I stood, strolled with a confident poise, and walked to the podium with a brilliant smile on my face and began to speak. From the responses of the audience, I had accomplished what I had planned. I was elated and felt redeemed because the valedictorian and salutatorian had to follow me in giving their presentation. I know it was not wise to boast about anything. Yet I was thrilled that I was a much better speaker than they were, and it showed that night.

I graduated on a Thursday and was on a Greyhound bus to Boston with my 16-year-old sister, Cassie, three days later. I had $5 in my pocketbook and was on my way to become a live-in maid for a family in Newton, MA. The fact that I did not know how to cook never entered my mind.

2

The Reality of Being Poor in a Big City

Cassie and I arrived in Boston on Tuesday and were met by our employers. As soon as our luggage had been retrieved, we were driven to their homes. The family I worked for had two daughters and one son. The son's name was Hank. My employers were the Millers. The two daughters were away at overnight camp, and the son was the only child remaining at home and attended day camp. Cassie and I never meant to remain as maids. We knew this was only a method we used to get us out of Alabama. Also, we knew to keep this fact to ourselves.

On my drive to the Millers' home, I was very nervous because I did not know what to expect. Since this was the first time I had ever been so far away from home, I was somewhat overwhelmed. During the ride to Mrs. Miller's house, I had very little to say, and I only responded with "yes, ma'am" or "no, ma'am" to Mrs. Miller's questions.

The first morning as a maid, Hank asked me to make him French toast for breakfast. I informed him that I did not know how to cook French toast, but if he described to me how to make some, I would cook it. I proceeded to follow his directions. Afterwards, Hank shared with his mother that the French toast I had cooked for him tasted strange. Mrs. Miller asked me what type of cooking oil had I used, and I told her it was vegetable cooking oil. She told me to use butter every time Hank wanted French toast for breakfast and that she would take care of all of the other meals.

My days off were Thursdays and Sundays. Two days after being in Massachusetts, I had my first Thursday off. Since I was unfamiliar with the public transportation system, Mrs. Miller drove me to Newton Centre and dropped me off. She told me to arrange to ride a taxi back to her home. Once Cassie arrived, we rode the trolley into Boston to Park Street Station. Since we had only worked as maids for two days, we could barely afford anything but lunch, which was pizza. This was the first time I had eaten pizza. The two slices were inexpensive but absolutely delicious.

On my first Sunday off, I joined Grant A.M.E. Church, which was located on Washington Street in Boston. The church was very accessible by riding the subway to Northampton Station. Since I had grown up in Alabama attending a Methodist church all my life, I continued this tradition. I wrote Mama telling her that I had joined a Methodist church, and she was very pleased.

As I attended Grant A.M.E. every Sunday, just as I had attended church every Sunday in Alabama, I decided to attend the youth meetings held at the church on Sunday afternoons. I was enjoying getting acquainted with many of the teenagers my age and their parents. The order of the worship services were very similar to those I had attended at my home church in Alabama. I was comfortable enough to share with some of the adult members that my sister Cassie and I would need to find a place to live no later than the first of September, because we would be leaving our live-in jobs and moving into Boston in the South End, find jobs, register, and attend school by then. Actually, I was praying and hoping a family would be willing to rent us a room in their home. Regrettably, no one came forward and offered to rent us a room, and I was very disappointed.

I developed a severe summer cold with chronic coughing during my first month in Newton. Mrs. Miller took me to her primary care physician (PCP) and paid for the visit. She deducted a portion of the bill each week from my salary until the debt was paid. My salary was $40 per week. Once a month, I sent $20 to Mama to pay for a washing machine she had purchased on time, and I saved a portion of my salary each week. Mrs. Miller was a kind woman and was not demanding at all. She would patiently teach me the things she wanted me to do. For instance, Mrs. Miller taught me how to polish her silverware, and she owned plenty of it. I was a fast learner.

My chores were not too difficult since I did not have to be concerned about cooking the dinners each day. I developed a daily routine for certain chores and weekly chores for others. I did not enjoy any of the chores though. However, it was the first time I had the convenience of using a modern washer and dryer, and the ironing space was almost as beautiful as the rest of the house. For the first time in my entire life, I had a beautiful room and bed all to myself. I even had a television in my room. I would daydream about one day I would live in a beautiful house and have a housekeeper who would cook meals for my family and me.

As the weeks rapidly passed, I didn't realize that summer camp was over for the two girls until Mr. and Mrs. Miller arrived home with them on a Sunday afternoon. Now I had to cook breakfast for three children, and they very seldom wanted the same foods. Hank wanted either French toast or cereal for breakfast, and I had become very good at making French toast. With the two girls, I never knew what to expect. Sometimes, I felt they just wanted to be difficult just to irritate me for no specific reason. For the life of me, I cannot recall their names. I do remember that one was age 13 and the other one was 11.

Basically, I was left alone to attend to my chores, even after all three children were home. Mrs. Miller was very busy organizing their school clothes and supplies for the upcoming school year. When she left home, the children accompanied her. I was not privy to their daily plans. And besides, I was not interested in any of them anyway.

Those summer months were passing by fast, and the money Cassie and I were saving were not adding up to much. Cassie needed to register for high school by September, and I needed to register for evening business classes. On one of our Thursdays off, Cassie and I went searching for an affordable apartment in the South End section of Boston. Since neither of us owned any furniture, we needed an affordable furnished apartment.

All of the furnished two-bedroom apartments were too expensive for us. As it turned out, our friend, Donna, wanted to quit her live-in job, too, and Cassie and I welcomed her and readily included her in our plans. The three of us realized that the only affordable furnished apartment that we could afford would be a furnished one-bedroom kitchenette apartment, and there were plenty of vacant ones on side streets.

As the month of September was fast approaching, I had not decided if I would give Mrs. Miller advance notice of my departure or not. When my first day off in the month of September came, I just packed all of my belongings, told Mrs. Miller I was quitting, and walked away without giving her a second thought. Therefore, Cassie, Donna and I left our jobs and moved into a furnished kitchenette apartment together. Donna was from Mobile, Alabama, and we had all met on one of our days off. She had recently graduated from high school, just like me, and had used the same method as we had used to escape from Alabama.

Since the three of us had never lived in a rented apartment of any kind before, our new living arrangements would take us some time getting used to. For instance, the bathroom was located at the end of the hallway on the same floor as our apartment. This was the first we had ever lived in a multi-family building and the first time any of us had to use a community bathroom for all of our personal and hygiene needs. We included bleach, Lysol, and sponges on our grocery list. We were on a tight budget, and all of us agreed to contribute the same amounts for groceries and rent.

Immediately, the three of us obtained jobs in a clothing factory that made raincoats. Our job was to check all raincoats and remove all excess threads. This 40-hour a week job paid us $1.25/hour. It was not much, but it was better than working as a maid, and it was much better than working in the cotton fields. After a few weeks, Donna left and went back to Alabama to attend nursing school, and Cassie and I started school in September at the Jeremiah E. Burke High School in Dorchester as planned. Cassie took classes needed to graduate from high school, and I took typing and shorthand classes in the evening in preparation for an office job in the near future.

As the end of September was only a few days away, Cassie and I realized that we were unprepared for the fall and winter in New England. Whereas the temperatures were relatively the same for the months of September and October in Alabama, September's temperature was already feeling like the temperature in Alabama in late November. Cassie and I decided to shop for winter coats, gloves, hats, and boots before it was too late. Due to our small savings, we had to put our coats, gloves, and hats on a lay-a-way plan, and we purchased winter boots outright.

As it turned out, our coats did not hold up well for the long New England winter of 1965-66 because of their poor quality. We had learned a valuable lesson from this experience and decided that we would plan better for the next winter and never buy cheap and poor-quality coats and boots ever again. First, we would shop at stores with better quality clothes, coats, and shoes. Second, we would use lay-a-way plans at these stores, if possible. To cover all bases, we decided that we would begin looking for sales of quality winter coats and boots months in advance of winter. As it turned out, Cassie and I were much better prepared for the followings winters.

Well, over the next several months, Cassie and I changed addresses and jobs so frequently that I cannot remember the locations of all of them or the names of all of those different jobs. The reasons we moved from one apartment to another and from one job to another were always the same. Every new furnished apartment was better in appearance, had its private bathroom, and was located either on a cleaner street or in safer neighbor with less traffic. Each new job paid a few cents more per hour. Cassie and I rode the public buses or subways to and from each job.

However, I do remember working at KLH in Cambridge and Jordan Marsh in downtown Boston, and I remember that we lived on different side streets off Columbus Avenue and Tremont Street in the South End. Also, I remember riding the public buses to and from both jobs.

Being young and carefree, Cassie and I met other young women and teenagers in our age group with similar backgrounds and became good friends. But we were not fortunate enough to meet decent young guys during our first year in Massachusetts. Therefore, we shied away from them after a couple of disappointments. Because we had to work to support ourselves in unsatisfactory jobs during the day and attend school at night, we had no time to waste trying to meet guys. But we thoroughly enjoyed going to school and socializing with our girlfriends.

My life was hard but never as hard as it had been in Alabama. Never once did I ever consider returning home to Alabama to stay. I knew that there was no future for me in Alabama. I was determined to make something out of myself in Massachusetts. I had entered Jeremiah E. Burke High School's evening program, so that I could obtain a better job. I felt an urgency to improve my employment options as soon as possible because I knew my aspiration of attending college would be delayed for at least two years. My typing and shorthand were absolutely terrible, and I made slow progress in them both. I did not own a typewriter and could not afford to purchase even a used one. Most of the other students in my typing class were able to practice at home between classes. I could not even practice at work because of the type of job I was doing. Nevertheless, I was determined to stay in Massachusetts and make something out of myself.

Although our jobs were nothing to boast about, Cassie and I enjoyed attending school. Since all of our friends had lousy jobs, we felt right at home complaining about our jobs to them, and they complained about their jobs to us. All of us were from similar backgrounds. We were all from a two parent home, had several siblings, had been raised in church, and recently graduated from high school. None of us had any skills that qualified us for higher paying jobs than we currently had. Therefore, all of us related to the difficulties of living in Boston and earning very little money from low paying jobs. And, we all were on tight budgets. Yet, we exhibited positive attitudes about our future. All of us believed in ourselves and our potentials and were willing to work hard to realize our goals. We understood that success meant different things to each of us, just as someone's trash could be someone else's treasure.

Cassie and I remained optimistic as we regularly searched for better paying jobs and better affordable furnished apartments. For a short period of time, Cassie and I moved in with a girlfriend named Estella who was from Tennessee. She graduated from high two years earlier, worked as a live-in maid for one year, and had been living alone in a furnished apartment for one year. I asked Estella if Cassie and I could share her apartment and pay her our equal portion of the rent. She readily agreed, and Cassie and I moved in with her immediately.

3

My Fears and Struggles

*A*lthough I was making slow progress in moving toward my goal of attending college full-time, nothing traumatic had ever happened to me during those several months after arriving in Massachusetts. In less than a year after arriving in Massachusetts, the most heinous, vile, and horrific thing that I could ever imagine happened to me.

Shockingly, I was raped by a man who had been introduced to me by a female acquaintance from my hometown. The acquaintance's name was Hattie. This young man was a friend of Hattie's husband. He was from a very large family and he had several young siblings. This young man was at least four years older than I was, and he and I had talked on a few occasions whenever I saw Hattie and her husband and him. On one of those occasions, he asked me if I were willing to help him babysit his younger siblings later. I agreed without thinking about any danger that might be waiting for me. Besides, I had plenty of experience babysitting my young siblings.

The rape that occurred that night after all of his younger siblings were asleep in bed was so devastating that I just wanted to die. As I wrestled with him, attempting to escape from his grip, I was screaming the words, *no, I don't want to!* He persisted and completed the act of rape. I, in turn, was devastated and wanted to die on the spot. I was in a state of unbelief and could not understand why this man had forced himself on me.

Somehow, I made it back to my apartment and called the police and reported the rape. Over the phone, the male police officer made me feel as if the rape was my fault, because I went over to his house. I tried to explain to the police officer that I only went to the man's home to help him babysit his younger siblings, because I had plenty of younger siblings and experience babysitting them. The police officer told me that this scenario would boil down to my word against his. I quickly hung up the phone and cried uncontrollably and constantly. I took a long hot tub bathe and attempted to fall asleep.

As I lay in bed, I thought about the attitude of the male police officer and about his comments to me. His comments had begun to make me feel guilty and ashamed. I partly blamed myself, in a way, because I felt that I should not have trusted him, and I should have not agreed to help him babysit his younger siblings. But I only agreed to help babysit. I actually wanted to just fall asleep and never awaken. I continued to cry constantly. I took several hot baths each day for several days. I was an emotional wreck and did not know what I was supposed to do.

At the age of 18, I was naïve and a late bloomer, and it had never occurred to me to consider this type of cruelty forced on anyone. I had been very focused and determined to get ahead in life by attending college by the time I was 20. Every night I prayed to God to allow me to sleep into eternity, but every morning God would awaken me. I questioned God, and I was very angry with God. I was perplexed and disturbed about why God had allowed such a heinous and horrific thing happen to me since I was trying to love God first and to love others as I love myself as my parents had taught me. My life was not turning out the way I had visualized.

Outwardly, I appeared whole and healthy. I hid my emotional, physical, and psychological pain very well from everyone. But inwardly, I was broken, ashamed, unworthy, unclean, unqualified, and inferior. I felt that I had disgraced my parents and myself as the result of the rape. I struggled in my relationship with God. I felt God did not love me as much as John 3:16 said. I felt God favored certain individuals, and I was not one of them. I purposely stopped praying to God daily because I felt God was not listening and did not care enough about me. My state of mind convinced me that it was all up to me to make my life better. Yes, to the world, I was functioning just fine, but I was spiritually dead. I allowed my membership at Grant A.M.E. Church to lapse. I ceased participating in all youth meetings; I stopped reading the Bible, and I stopped praying daily. My pain was almost unbearable. I became very depressed, sad, and introverted. And I continued praying to God to end my life. If God answered my prayers, God's answers were not the way I wanted them to be.

I moved into a small furnished rear apartment, which consisted of a bedroom with a separate kitchen and bathroom. My rent was $75/month with utilities included. I could not afford a telephone or television. However, I did have a small radio. Cassie got married. I, in turn, had discovered that I was pregnant by the man who had raped me. I did not know what to do. I had pregnancy sickness every day for the first trimester. I lost weight, and I still did not know what I was going to do. My baby continued to grow inside of my womb. I felt that I was living a horrible and cruel nightmare 24/7.

One day, Cassie said to me that she wished this heinous act had happened to her rather than me. I did not quite understand what she meant, but I sensed that Cassie felt that she could handle the situation better than I could. Cassie was suffering right along for me and with me and wished that she could take some of my pain and agony away. She realized that this rape had almost taken away my will to live.

During this time, I am so very grateful to Cassie for being there supporting me through it all and patiently listening and encouraging me, even on my worst days. Somehow, I decided that I wanted to live. Also, I decided that I would have my baby and keep it. I was determined to grow a healthy baby, be the best mother as possible to my baby, and become what I desired to be. Besides, I was only 18-years-old, and a young woman with the potentials of a great future. Although I did not know what the future held, I still believed in myself.

I changed jobs once again but for different reasons than all of the other times. I did not want to see anyone I knew before the rape. I even borrowed a wedding ring from a woman who was divorced. I introduced myself to all of my new co-workers as being married; my husband was stationed in Vietnam, and he was a private in the Army. I talked, sang, and read happy books to my baby on a regular basis. I hoped my baby was a girl. I made efforts to remain upbeat and positive.

During my daily walks, I described what I saw around me to my growing baby. If I did not feel like walking, I explained to my baby that it was not her fault that I felt uninspired and that together we would get through this exercise.

I was used to being alone when I read books, and I still enjoyed this pastime. But this was different. I was very lonely during my pregnancy. My entire personality changed. I smiled less and less as my pregnancy progressed, and I was depressed much of the time, although I tried to convince myself that I was not. I just wanted the nine and a half months to move along faster and to be done with being pregnant. I felt like I was serving a prison sentence, which I did not deserve. This pregnancy had taken over my entire life, and I did not have the security or the parenting skills I felt that I needed to raise a baby. I felt as if it was me against the entire world, and often times I felt that the world would win.

A month before my due date, I had gone to the welfare office and applied for Medicaid benefits so that I would receive a bi-weekly check to pay my rent and food for my baby and me. The social worker authorized a voucher for a baby crib and mattress. I went to Salvation Army and purchased both of these items there. I was told that I would receive $72 bi-weekly beginning December 15th. I had a little savings, which I used to purchase diapers, newborn onesies, and other baby items. I could not afford a high chair or stroller. I did not mind, though. I never told anyone that I would be receiving a welfare check twice a month while I was unable to work. I was very embarrassed to be on welfare, because I had worked hard all my life and never relied on the government for anything in my entire life, since I am a descendant of hard-working people who relied on God and their own hard work to live

I avoided reading horror books or seeing horror movies. I continued to do a lot of walking on a daily basis throughout my pregnancy. I was alone the majority of the time, except when I visited Cassie and Arola.

I worked up until one week before my due date. Four days before my due date, I began experiencing labor pains around 10:00 PM on December 26th. I took a taxi to the emergency room at Boston City Hospital around 6:00 AM on December 27th. The emergency room physician told me that it would be several hours before I would give birth to my baby, and since I lived alone and was so young that it would be best if I were admitted into the hospital. I agreed to be admitted.

Since all of my prenatal appointments had been at Boston City Hospital, my medical records were readily accessible to all pertinent medical personnel and my admission into the hospital went smoothly. I was taken directly to the maternity ward, prepped, examined by the assigned physician, and given a mild sedative to help me relax and sleep. At 7:00 PM on December 27th, I awoke in excruciating pains and cried out loudly for help. The assigned nurse immediately was at my bedside, accessed my situation, and paged for the assigned physician. Five minutes after I had awoken, and after 21 hours of labor, I gave birth to a seven pound and 12 ounce baby girl. I named her Angela because she was my angel, and because she had given me back the will to live for her and myself. Angela was four days earlier than expected, and I was relieved.

During my stay in the hospital, I took breastfeeding instructions. But every time Angela sucked my nipple, I tensed up because I was unable to tolerate the pain. Finally, the nurse brought Angela to me and handed me a bottle filled with formula milk. The nurse instructed me in the proper ways to feed and burp Angela. Once I had mastered this, I was instructed on bathing and changing diapers. Four days after giving birth to Angela, I took a taxi back to my apartment with my angel in my arms.

Raising a newborn baby all alone was not easy. I often wished I had Mama living with me or at least an older woman there to help me through it all. Every feeding, diaper change, and bathe was my responsibility. I was even unsure whether I was burping Angela correctly after each feeding, and I was afraid to lie her down in her crib. During the first year, I would constantly get up throughout the night checking to see if Angela was still breathing. I carried Angela in my arms everywhere. I saw other mothers with their babies in strollers. But I did not mind the fact that I could not afford a stroller for Angela, because my baby girl could feel my heart beats and arms around her. I would sit for hours holding Angela as she slept, and I was not concerned if I spoiled her for holding her too much. I believed that if I spoiled her with my love, she would grow up knowing that her mother loved her, regardless of how she was conceived.

Due to limited finances, at no time did Angela have more than three complete outfits that fit during the first three years of her life, and I only purchased her one pairs of shoes at a time. I would always wash the soiled clothes she had worn each day by hand at night before I retired. In this way, Angela always had two clean and ready to wear outfits for each day. Sometimes, Angela would need two outfits daily.

Six weeks after giving birth, my physician informed me that I was recovered enough to work. Soon after my postnatal checkup, I obtained a file clerk's job at Kemper Insurance Company, which was located in downtown Boston on Tremont Street. I notified the welfare office that I had obtained a job as a file clerk. My salary was $60/week, and the office was clean and bright. I was told by the social worker that I would be receiving at least two or three more checks before being removed from the program. I returned the wedding ring to its rightful owner. Arola agreed to be my daughter's childcare provider while I worked.

I enjoyed the work, and the people were very kind and friendly. I made a very good friend at work by the name of Diane. She was from Virginia and had come to Boston once she had graduated from high school just as I had done. We became a twosome and enjoyed being together. I shared my past experiences with her and introduced her to my baby daughter. Diane was engaged to Frankie, the son of a minister and pastor of a local church. They were Pentecostal.

Diane invited me to her home church, and I readily accepted her invitation. I enjoyed the entire service and met many friendly and kind people there. This was the first time I had set foot inside of a church since before Angela was borne. Diane's home church had many little children for Angela to play with. Although I found comfort in attending church, I did not seek any reconciliatory relationship with God. I enjoyed the fellowship and conversations with the church members and was very comfortable being with them. But I could not see or feel the comfort of God. At this juncture, I did not seek God or any relationship with God, because I still felt that God had failed me. However, I thoroughly enjoyed the singing and being with people. We shared good conversations, good foods, and much laughter together.

After a period of time, Arola and I moved into an apartment together in Jamaica Plains, not far from Green

Street Subway Station. The apartment was on a quiet street and in a relatively safe neighborhood. I engaged an older woman who lived across the street to be Angela's childcare provider. Because many years have passed, I cannot recall the name of Angela's new childcare provider. However, she had already raised her children and was a grandmother. She was just the right person to take care of Angela and help me improve my parenting skills. I was receptive to all of her advice, and she only charged me ten dollars each week. Instantly, I realized that she was not providing childcare of Angela for the money. She recognized that I needed help, and she was part of my village. I was very grateful to be included and the recipient of her love.

Several months after attending Diane's home church, I began to attend Methodist and Baptist churches again, but only occasionally, and very rarely the same church in the same month. When I attended these different churches, Angela was taken to children's church each Sunday. With Angela in children church, I was able to relax and enjoy the entire worship service without being distracted. The church choirs made joyful noises to God through songs and the gifted musicians made joyful noises to God through their music. I had begun to look forward to Sundays again. Angela, to her benefit, had many playmates in children church. She and her playmates were never ready to leave when the worship services ended, because they were thoroughly enjoying themselves. The children ministry effectively taught the little children all of the Biblical stories and principles through creative graphic art illustrations and participations. Angela proudly showed and told me what she had done in children church each Sunday.

Attending church was beneficial for Angela and me, and the Biblical teaching Angela was receiving provided opportunities for her to learn about the only begotten Son of God, Jesus Christ. I honestly did not want my issues with God to hinder Angela's opportunities to discover God's plans for her life, and the children's church ministry had a tremendous influence on Angela's overall growth and development.

Although Cassie was busy being a wife, working a full-time job, and attending school, she remained my closest friend and confidant. One Sunday afternoon after church, I went to visit Cassie and was told by her husband that Cassie was visiting her girlfriend, Fluorine, at her home. Angela was with me. I went directly to Fluorine's house and Cassie was there. There were several girls and guys there. I did not know anyone but Cassie. I was introduced to several girls and guys who were from the same hometown as Fluorine. I did not attempt to be very friendly with any of the guys, because my purpose was primarily to visit with Cassie. After a couple of hours of friendly conversation, I decided to leave and go back to the apartment I shared with Arola. I gathered Angela in my arms and walked the four blocks to the nearest subway station. I found out later that there had been a young man at Fluorine's house who watched Angela and me as we crossed the street. It had been Robert, and he remembered that I had worn a beautiful green dress.

The following Saturday, Cassie invited me to go dancing with her and girlfriends. It was a local club located on Tremont Street where young adults went to dance and socialize. Cassie and a group of her friends were standing outside of this local club waiting for me to arrive. There were at least eight of them. As I was greeting everyone, one of the young men I had been briefly introduced to on the previous Sunday walked over and introduced himself. He said his name was Robert and that we had met on Sunday at Fluorine's house. This was when Robert told me that he had watched me as I had crossed the street, wearing a beautiful green dress and protectively carrying my baby in my arms.

I had fun that night being around people my own age, dancing, laughing, and enjoying each other's company. All of the young women were under the age of 21, and we were not drinking any alcoholic beverages. Well, I know for sure Cassie and I were not. My favorite drink was a Shirley Temple with extra cherries.

Growing up in a small southern town, it was customary to see two girls dancing together and a group of girls dancing together. Usually, my friends and I would teach each other new dance steps at birthday and school parties. After a few hours, some of the guys began to ask the girls to dance. Robert walked over to me, asked me to dance, and I accepted. Robert asked permission to escort me home. I said yes. Around 11:00 PM, I said goodnight to Cassie and her friends, and Robert and I walked to the subway train station.

As Robert and I were riding the subway, Robert asked me for a movie date. I enjoyed going to the movies, and so I accepted. We made arrangements to go to a matinee movie on Sunday. I had never gone to an evening movie, so it never occurred to me to suggest going to an evening movie or that Robert expected to take me to a movie in the evening. During our conversation, I said I would be ready to go to a four o'clock movie. Robert arrived at my sister's and my apartment promptly, as promised on that Sunday.

We walked the few blocks to the subway train station and rode to downtown Boston. The movie theatre was on Washington Street and only a few blocks from the subway station. A James Bond movie was playing. I liked watching James Bond movies, and so I was very pleased with Robert's selection. All of the James Bond movies were entertaining to me and very enjoyable. None of them were to be taken seriously. For me, watching them was strictly an opportunity to enjoy and relax.

During the movie, Robert attempted to kiss me on my lips. Fortunately for me, I caught a glimpse of him in the corner of my right eye moving toward my face, which allowed me time to move my face to the left. Robert's kiss landed on my right cheek. Robert was very surprised that I had moved my head to prevent him from kissing me on my lips. He asked me why I moved my head, and I told him that I did not kiss strangers, and I never allowed myself to be kissed on a first date. I sensed that he was somewhat perplexed, but we continued to watch the movie.

The following week, every time I turned around, Robert was calling me every night and asking me for a second date. Although I took his calls, I hesitated about a second date. He pursued me relentlessly, as if he was driven as by an uncontrollable power. Initially, I did not take him seriously. I was very untrusting of the opposite sex because of my previous experience when I was 18-years-old. I also assumed that he felt a slight rejection when we were at the movies and his ego had been hurt and was attempting to have his own way. But when Robert continued to call each night and sounded sincere, I decided to go out with him again.

As it turned out, Robert was fun to go out with. He had a great sense of humor and had embraced a carefree attitude. Robert told funny jokes, which caused me to laugh and relax in his presence. We would hold hands as we ran down the street to catch the MBTA bus, laughing the entire time. I, on the other hand, was more serious and not a good joke teller. We were complete opposites. We laughed together a lot. I did not know that Robert did not make much money at the time because he paid for everything on our dates. Whether it was dinner and a movie or whether we spent the day at Revere Beach, Robert paid for everything. And I enjoyed every minute when we were together. He was very protective, and he did everything in his power to please me and to insure that I had a good time on our dates. Robert had a habit of holding my hand as we walked together; he would open doors and help me with my coat and he would help me with my chair. Robert was a southern gentleman, as Daddy would say. I must admit, I was very impressed with his behavior.

Initially, I did not include Angela on any of my dates with Robert. I did not want her to become attached to him, if he were not a keeper. After a few dates, Robert began to urge me to bring Angela with us and we would plan our dates around things Angela would enjoy. Franklin Park Zoo was one of Angela's favorite places to visit. We spent lots of Saturday afternoons at the zoo, Boston Commons, and movies. We saw every Walt Disney movie playing in the theaters and more than once.

After dating for three months, I knew Robert was a keeper and our relationship moved to another level. Robert and I had discussed marriage on several occasions, but we were still young. So marriage was something that we would plan for in the future. Robert and I did not know how not to get pregnant, and I was frantic each month until my period came. We were using over the counter (OTC) birth control, which was rather messy. I believe from Robert's viewpoint that we could have continued dating for years without getting married, although we were behaving intimately together as if we were married.

By the time we had been dating six months, I was ready to discuss marriage seriously, and I decided that if we were going to get married, it had to be as soon as possible. To be honest, I did not want to get pregnant ever again, and I needed to be married in order to get a prescription for birth control. Traditionally unmarried African American girls and women did not ask doctors for prescriptions for birth control. If they did, I was totally unaware of it. Besides, I would have been too ashamed to admit to anyone that I was sexually active with Robert. Just knowing God knew was already bad enough.

On a very cold December day in 1968, as Robert and I walked to the subway station, I asked him, "When are we getting married?" Robert said any time I wanted to. I immediately said all right and suggested March 1969. As soon as I had an opportunity, I looked at a 1969 calendar and chose March 8th. March 8th was a day before Daddy's birthday. In addition, I chose a March wedding date just in case I got pregnant in the meantime and knew I would not be showing a pregnancy by then. As I stated before, Robert and I had no idea how not to become pregnant.

Since Robert and I had very little money saved and our parents were not financially able to help us, our wedding plans were kept very simple. Therefore, our wedding plans were a no brainer. Of course, I would purchase a new outfit; Robert would purpose a new black suit. We arranged for family members and friends to cook the various dishes for the reception. And our wedding plans were announced via phone calls and word of mouth. There were only Cassie and four other people invited to the wedding.

Robert had never joined any church, although he had attended a Baptist church on a regular basis while living in Mississippi with his parents and paternal grandmother. I had grown up in a Methodist Church since I was a baby. Robert was very adamant that he would not get married in a Methodist Church. Robert shared with me that for generations the Howards had been Baptist, and he was not going to change this tradition. I did not argue with him. However, I pointed out that he had never joined any church; he had never been baptized, and therefore, he was not a Baptist. Robert said that this did not matter because he still did not want to be associated with any church other than a Baptist one.

I asked, "Robert, why you never joined any church?"

He responded, "I never saw a miraculous event." I pondered on what Robert had just told me and thought to myself that some believers make it very complicated for others to believe and accept Jesus Christ as Savior. I did not want to criticize Robert's upbringing. Besides, I had been raised in the church for 17 years, and where had it gotten me?

I had an open mind and knew that Baptist and Methodist churches used similar Bibles. In my hometown, which was similar to most small southern towns, churches held Sunday worship services twice a month and three times whenever there were fifth Sundays. On the remaining Sundays, church members attended other churches. This approach allowed relationships to develop and strengthen in the community. Everyone knew each other.

Robert and I decided to go see the pastor of New Hope Baptist Church, which was located on Harrison Avenue in Boston at the time. His name was Rev. Dubois. After talking with us, asking us questions, and mulling over our responses, Rev. Dubois agreed to marry us on Saturday, March 8, 1969 at 6:00 PM.

I went and purchased a new outfit from one of those very exclusive and expensive stores located on Boylston Street. Up until then, I had never paid more than $50 for a dress. Robert and I went shopping for his new black suit. Then, Robert and I went to apply for a marriage license. Once we arrived at Boston City Hall, Robert confessed that he had lied about his age. I was stunned to discover that Robert was not two years older than me, but I was a year than older than he.

Doubt began to creep in my mind, and I began to doubt Robert's character, honesty, and sincerity about many things. His explanation was that he believed I would have not agreed to go out with him if I had known that he was younger than I. I was not impressed with his explanation, and I decided to go home. I had been truthful about my past experiences, even including the heinous rape I had survived. I wanted Robert to understand why I felt the way I did about everything, even premarital sex before we were serious about each other. He, on the other hand, had been deceptive about his age lead me to wonder what other things he had been deceptive about. My trust in Robert was waning by the second.

Robert continued to apologize to me for being dishonest and assured me that this was the only thing he was not truthful about. Since I loved him, I agreed to accompany him to Boston City Hall for our marriage license and obtain our blood tests, although I had lingering doubts about many things.

On Saturday, March 8th, it was very cold in New England. Robert, Rev. Dubois, and the few invited guests waited patiently at New Hope Baptist Church. When I failed to show by 5:45 PM, Robert began to wonder whether I was going to be a no show bride. At 6:15 PM, I arrived at the church and gave him no explanation for being late. There were two major reasons I arrived late at New Hope Baptist Church. First, I had begun to have cold feet. Marriage was a very serious undertaking, and I only wanted to get married once in my lifetime. I began to ask myself if I should take the chance on Robert. Second, after making up my mind to go through with the wedding, there was not enough time remaining for me to make it to the church on time.

As it turned out, one of Robert's co-workers escorted me down the aisle. We exchanged marriage vows and proceeded directly to our wedding reception. I had invited all of Robert's female friends to the reception so that none of them would honestly say they did not know we were married.

We took off Monday from work. On Tuesday, Robert and I returned to work and continued our normal routine. Although I had cooked one dinner for Robert before we got married, which did not turn out very well, Robert soon discovered that I really did not know how to cook. Robert would jokingly say he did not marry me for my cooking, but he had married me for my sexy legs.

I remember on one occasion that Robert had asked me to cook him some pinto beans and ham hocks. The outcome would have been different, I believe, if Robert would have asked me to cook something that I had seen Mama prepare or at least I had eaten before. I was familiar with ham hocks, but I had never eaten or seen any pinto beans. Evidently, they were dried beans. I had never seen Mama prepare or cook dried beans. For the first 11 years, I lived on a farm where we grew our vegetables and had peaches, plums, and pears growing on trees. And even after Daddy stopped sharecropping, Mama maintained a vegetable garden every year and canning continued each summer. I don't remember Mama or Daddy ever buying any pinto beans or any kind of dried beans and peas. Now Robert was asking me to cook something that I was totally unfamiliar with. Robert, Angela and I went to A&P Supermarket for the pinto beans and ham hocks. Robert located the pinto beans and ham hocks.

While Robert was working one Saturday, I decided to cook the pinto beans and ham hocks. When Robert arrived home, he said, "Something smells good in the kitchen." I must admit, the ham hocks and pinto beans gave off a pleasant aroma. I fixed Robert's plate and he began to eat and bit down on something very hard. When Robert removed the food from his mouth, he found small rocks. Robert looked at me and asked, "Did you pick the beans and wash them before cooking them?"

I asked, "How can I pick beans when they are already picked and were in a plastic bag? And *no*, I did not wash them because I thought them were already clean." Robert shook his head, laughed, and began to explain what he meant by picking the pinto beans first and then washing them several times before placing them in the cooking pot.

Another time Robert asked me to bake him a cake from scratch. After Robert left for work on a Saturday, Angela and I went shopping for the ingredients needed for the cake, including the chocolate frosting. I did not have an electric mixer, but I did own a hand beater. After mixing all of the ingredients together with the hand beater, I had blisters on my left hand, which were very painful. When Robert arrived home from work later that day, he took one look at the cake and smiled. The cake looked delicious to him. He picked up a knife and tried to slice him a piece. The knife would not penetrate that cake. Robert looked up at me, laughed, and shook his head. Then he wrapped the cake in newspaper and threw it in the trash.

Later, Robert said, "Please don't bake a cake for me anymore." Well, I agreed to Robert's request and never attempted to bake a cake from scratch ever again. However, all of my cakes turned out well when I used Hines and Betty Crocker cake mixes.

Another time Robert wanted me to cook ox tails and lima beans for him. I never heard of anyone eating ox tails before until Robert mentioned them. Well, the results were disastrous again.

Robert said, "Please don't cook me anymore ox tails and lima beans ever again." Since Angela and I were not going to eat any ox tails and lima beans, Robert had enough left over for at least three additional meals. He struggled while eating the leftovers because the ox tails and lima beans were not cooked the way he was accustomed to eating them.

Reflecting back, I realize God brought a wonderful person into my life to help me through the heinous experience of being raped. Robert has remained a strong and compassionate man who affirmed me as a phenomenal woman. He is still my husband and the love of my life. My daughter became Robert's daughter. He adopted her during the first month after we were married, and all of the blank spaces that were on her birth certificate were filled in. Robert is the only father our daughter has ever known, and they both absolutely love each other. I was very fortunate and blessed after all. Our daughter grew into a beautiful, healthy, and happy baby girl. On weekends, the three of us would go to Franklin Park on picnics and enjoy visiting the animals in the zoo.

In the meantime, I continued working at Kemper Insurance Company and was promoted to a coding clerk. This job paid a little more money and offered overtime. I took advantage of all of the overtime that was available to me. During the next few years, I attended several different business schools at night and took refresher courses in preparation to attend college as I soon I could.

As my life was filled with challenges, they were all for the good of my family and me. I would clean our apartment thoroughly every Friday night. Robert and I could not afford a washer and dryer or a car. So, every Saturday morning after Robert left for work, I would take Angela with me to the supermarket. Robert and I had budgeted 40 dollars for weekly groceries, and I always took my grocery list with me. Angela and I would ride the MBTA bus to the supermarket and used a person who would charge less than a taxi to take us home. During that period in time, it was a common practice for adult car owners to gather in the supermarket parking lots for the sole purpose of earning extra money.

Once Angela and I arrived at the supermarket, Angela would walk ahead of me and do her own shopping as I looked for items on my list that might be on sale. Then, at the cash register, I would discover several items in the cart that were not on my grocery list. I had no other choice but to remove each one of them. Of course, Angela protested each time, but I could not afford to pay for these extra items. However, I do recall that for a brief time I was fortunate to know one of the cashiers who would ring up my groceries for far less. During this brief period, all of the items Angela had chosen remained in my cart.

After Angela and I arrived home from the supermarket, and after I had put all of the grocery items away, we proceeded to walk to the laundromat. This was the routine every Saturday. After the clothes were washed and folded, we walked back to our apartment, and I put the clothes away in their proper places. Then I began to cook dinner, so that my cooking would not interfere with our afternoon plans. Usually, it was a trip to the zoo or an afternoon movie. Often times Robert would go out with one of his male friends later.

As I looked forward to the day when I would realize my goal of being a doctor, I never lost my desire to attend Tufts University School of Dental Medicine one day. I had decided that I would become a dentist rather than a physician. My decision was based on the fact that I did not want to have to deal with death and dying on a routine basis. Oddly enough, years later, I chose to take an independent college course and chose as my topic "death and dying."

When Robert and I had first met, he stated that one day he would like to become an auto body repairman and maybe own his business one day. When we got married, he was just working in a factory earning $106 per week after taxes were withheld. I was bringing home $96 bi-weekly after taxes were withheld. We would combine our paychecks; we would take a portion from each paycheck for the rent and groceries, and we would set aside money for our commuting cost.

Some weeks we had less than ten dollars left over for recreation. With those few dollars, we would attend matinee movies a couple times per month. In those days, we each paid $1.50 to see two different movies. I had already purchased snacks and had placed them in my pocketbook before entering the movie theaters. Therefore, beverages were the only items we purchased at the movie counters.

After about six months into our marriage, I decided to check out some programs for auto body repairmen since Robert had said he would like to become one. Once I located a suitable program, I brought the application home; I helped him complete it, and he mailed it off. Robert was accepted to this vocational school in East Boston and arranged with his current employer to work part-time.

With Robert working part-time, our incomes drastically decreased. So, I began to work more overtime on my job whenever I could and attended business school on the other nights. Life still presented many challenges. Nevertheless, my life was better and I was happier.

Robert and I became very close friends with another couple, Maxine and her husband, Johnny. I had met

Maxine the first summer I arrived in Massachusetts. She had recently graduated from high school just as I had, and she was from Alabama, also. We had hit it off immediately. They had two boys. Johnny and Maxine owned a car. We would invite each other to our apartment for dinner and table games. In this way, we did not have to spend money on babysitters. Our children would be in another room playing, and when it was bedtime, Maxine and I would put them to bed. The children wore their pajamas to each other's apartment.

On other occasions, the four of us and our children would take in drive-in movies. We always dressed our children in their pajamas before going to the drive-in theatres, and all three were usually asleep before the second feature started. This was another great way to enjoy ourselves without spending much money.

On Sundays, when we all decided not to attend church, we would drive to Benson's Farm in Hudson, New Hampshire and Canobie Lake Park in Salem, New Hampshire. On these outings, Maxine and I had prepared foods for our lunch. The only thing we bought was ice cream. I had an insatiable appetite for ice cream and all flavors were my favorite during this juncture of my life. Because of my insatiable appetite for ice cream,

I routinely ate two quarts of ice cream a day. During those days, I never gained any weight or even thought about my weight because I was very active every day.

As Robert and I were busy with life and its responsibilities, Robert completed the program in nine months rather than a year. He was just that motivated to learn auto body repair and to move on using the skills he had acquired. During Robert's first job interview, he was hired at Auto City in East Boston. Finally, Robert had begun to make a living wage; we began to save a portion each week, and we began to enjoy going to a matinee movie each week.

After a year of working at Auto City, Robert decided that he wanted us to move to Los Angeles, California. I did not want to move. To me, Massachusetts was the educational mecca of the United States and of the entire world. I did know much about California and had no desire to live there. I definitely did not want to live in Watts, California, since I had seen terrible things on television and read about many horrible things in the newspapers about Watts.

There had been riots there and people being injured and killed during those riots. In addition, there were widespread rumors of police brutality. I remembered specifically that residents in Watts had accused the police officers of brutality, unfairness, and injustices. Certain areas of metropolitan Boston had experienced riots while I had been in Massachusetts. Although far from ideal, I was familiar with the environment in Massachusetts. Robert assured me that we would not be living in Watts. Even so, I did not want to move with him to California. It took several lengthy conversations with Mama to convince me to go to California with Robert.

Robert and Johnny drove to California while Maxine and I remained behind along with our children. This allowed time for our husbands to rent an apartment for us and become gainfully employed – we hoped. I arranged a verbal agreement with Shirley, Maxine's sister, to take over the monthly payments on Robert and my furniture at Summerville Furniture Store in Boston. Maxine and I flew out with our children a month later as planned to Los Angeles. Maxine and I were unsure what it would be like to live on the West Coast. I cannot speak for Maxine, but I was attempting to make the best out of this move, although I had a heavy heart and doubts.

Robert had rented a beautiful one-bedroom apartment. Palm trees lined both side of the street, not only on the street our apartment was located, but there were palm trees on every street. All of the lawns were perfectly cared for with beautiful and colorful flowers. I was surrounded by beauty. There was a playground in the middle of the apartment complex. I was very pleased with the location of the playground since our daughter was only three-years-old. Robert had found a job immediately upon arriving in Los Angeles.

Now it was up to me to find a satisfactory day care program for our daughter that we both like, and then to find a job. I chose a day care program that was located a couple blocks near our apartment mainly because of its proximity to our apartment and to a park. I interviewed at several different insurance companies, and each one of them required that I take a comprehensive written exam. Finally, I was hired at Firemen's Funds Insurance on Wilshire Boulevard in Los Angeles as a coding clerk. I was only making a weekly salary that was slightly more than my salary had been in Massachusetts. Yet our living expenses were far more than they had been in Massachusetts.

Although I was living in West Los Angeles in a beautiful and relatively safe neighborhood, I did not like living in California. Everything I needed to buy and places I needed go were very far apart from each other. Robert and I had no car. I rode two buses to work each day. Then I had to ride two buses back home. On my way home, I stopped and picked up Angela. I rode a bus to and from the supermarket. The only people we knew were Johnny and Maxine. It was very difficult for Robert and me to travel about to meet people since we did not know where to go. Maxine introduced us to her brother and sister-in-law. Now Robert and I knew four people in California. They invited us to their house party one Saturday night.

During the party, there was a long line of people waiting to use the bathroom, so I just took my proper place and waited, too. When it was my turn to go inside the bathroom, the person leaving the bathroom just handed me a marijuana joint. I took it and stared at it, as I wondered what to do with it.

Within a few seconds, the person standing immediately behind said, "He'll take it." I thought to myself, what type of house party was this? A few minutes later, I found Robert and told him what had happened. Robert just shrugged his shoulders and continued enjoying the party. I was thinking to myself that if the police raided this party, Robert and I would be guilty by association and not because we were smoking marijuana.

I shared my concerns with Robert and finally he agreed to take me home, although grudgingly. I never accepted another invitation to Maxine's brother and sister-law's parties.

A short time later, our friends, Johnny and Maxine, moved out of the neighborhood to a larger apartment, and Robert and I moved upstairs to a two-bedroom apartment. Now Robert and I knew no one in the neighborhood. We did not locate a suitable church in the neighborhood to attend since there was no Baptist church close by. Robert would only attend Baptist churches. Therefore, the entire time we lived in California, we never stepped inside of a church.

After a couple of months had passed, Robert and I decided to send Angela to live with his eldest sister in Mississippi, because we did not like the day care program she was attending. Besides, his sister was a principal of a preschool and kindergarten school, and we had complete confidence that Angela would receive all the love, care, nourishment, and education she needed.

Robert and I, on the other hand, struggled to make a go in our new place of residence. It was very difficult for us to meet the kind of people we desired to become friends with. I could not figure out the reason for this. It was as if we were from a different planet. There were topless bars all over the place in downtown Los Angeles, and everywhere it seemed. Since we did not own a car, we had to ride buses everywhere we went. I admitted to Robert that I regretted agreeing to the move and that I would be leaving going back to Massachusetts soon if things did not change.

It was difficult to locate suitable movie theaters. On one occasion, Maxine and I mistakenly ended up in a pornographic movie on a Saturday afternoon. As we were walking into the movie theater, we wondered why there were only men sitting in the theatrical seats. After settling in our seats, we looked at the screen and were shocked. We quickly left the theater and were glad that we knew no one and no one knew us.

Before we had a chance to finalize plans to send Angela to her aunt, an earthquake occurred. I woke up while the earthquake was happening and asked Robert what was going on. He said it was an earthquake.

Then I asked him, "What should we do?"

He said, "Nothing." I panicked and screamed without thinking about the affect my screaming and hysterics were having on Angela. I lost all composure and cried. I was terrified.

Robert had to comfort us both. I had completely lost my composure, and I imagined the ground opening up and falling into a bottomless pit. My imagination had gotten the best of me. For days I was very fearful of the worst, which never happened, although aftershocks continued for days. Robert and I made the final arrangements for Angela's departure by plane and sent her to Mississippi where she would be met by her paternal aunt.

Since I had lived in Alabama for the first 17 years of my life, I was very familiar with narrow-minded people. I had experienced some racial discrimination and exclusivity while living in Massachusetts. However, there were still many opportunities available to me in Massachusetts that I did not spend my days thinking about the narrow-mindedness of others, but rather I chose to think about taking advantage of the abundant opportunities. I was totally unprepared for California. Although I was considered an introvert when first meeting people, they soon discovered that I was actually an extrovert after a few minutes of conversation with me. But at work, I just did not fit in anywhere. I disliked my job tremendously. There were only two individuals I enjoyed talking with because we shared some commonalities. Both of them were much older than I, and I thoroughly enjoyed listening to them and asking lots of questions. I believed they enjoyed talking to me.

Except for the two older individuals, all of my other co-workers and I had nothing in common. I had learned at an early age that when people are nice rather than kind, those people are not genuine. The word "nice" describes things and places. The word "kind" describes people and is a condition of the human heart. The majority of white people I had come in contact with during the first 17 years of my life were very mean spirited toward me. The best of them were at least nice on their good day or bad day, but they were never kind. A person can fake niceness, since it does not express true feelings of the heart. A person cannot fake kindness, because kindness comes from the heart. One can feel the kindness expressed, see the kindness in one's eyes, and experience the kindness in one's body language. Kindness embraces kindness. My two older co-workers were kind to me every day, and all of the others were just nice to me every day.

Once Angela was in Mississippi, I began to make plans to move back to Massachusetts. I am not one to make major decisions quickly. I thought about the things I did not like and what to do about them. I was not consciously aware that I was actually praying to

God. However, I did realize that God knew all of my thoughts, desires, shortcomings, and potentials.

After I had made up my mind that I was moving back to Massachusetts, I discussed my plans with Robert. I very clearly told him that I was willing to move back with or without him but hopefully with him. He asked me to give him six months to straighten out everything.

While I was waiting for the six months to pass, I was asked by my supervisor to appear in an advertisement for Fireman's Fund Insurance Company. I was elated about being asked and for the opportunity. I was given a brief script to learn and was told to wear hot pants on the day the ad would be filmed. Well, I only had one pair of shorts that I thought would pass for hot pants.

On the day of the filming, I was very nervous. My nervousness surprised me, because I thought that I had conquered being very nervous before a performance. Evidently, I had not. The filming crew had me repeat my script numerous times and each one was just as bad as the previous ones. Finally, they gave up on me, and I never heard about whether the ad was made with another person or not. I do know, however, that I was never asked to appear in another Fireman's Fund Insurance Company's ad.

Another unsuccessful venture occurred while I waited for those six months to pass. I decided that I would make myself new outfits to wear to work. I rented a sewing machine, and I went shopping for dress fabrics and dress patterns. I chose dress patterns that did not appear too complicated. At night, I would spread the fabric on the kitchen floor, because it was the only floor that was big enough and was not carpeted. Since I had been taught sewing and how to a read dress pattern when I was in the eighth-grade, I thought this venture would be an easy feat for me.

In total, I made six dresses, and I was very pleased with them, except I had trouble sewing the zipper on each one. I began wearing my new homemade dresses to work and several of my co-workers complemented me on them.

Then it dawned on me that after each of my co-workers had complimented me that they all had asked, "Did you make your dress?" It took me about eight weeks to realize that my dresses actually looked home-made rather than store bought.

Finally, five months had passed, and I had only one more month to wait before my departure from Califor-nia. So, we notified Robert's sister in Mississippi to put

Angela on a plane to Los Angeles, and she did. Exactly one month later, the three of us were on a Greyhound bus traveling back to Massachusetts. Living in California had been such a great burden for me, and now that burden had been lifted. In my mind, I said goodbye to California and hello to Massachusetts. I imagined a great future was waiting for the three of us in Massachusetts.

I was very excited about returning to Massachusetts, because I still considered Massachusetts to be the educational mecca of the world. I maintained my belief that I could accomplish all of my educational goals in Massachusetts. The bus trip was almost unbearable, because I had motion sickness during the entire trip. Usually, my bouts with motion sickness had been minor whenever I had ridden buses. But traveling through Arizona and New Mexico almost got the best of me because the temperatures were far above 110-degree Fahrenheit. And I felt as if the air conditioner was not functioning properly. Even at age four, Angela felt the heat and complained regularly. I was so miserable from motion sickness and the heat that I felt as if I would be better off dead at the time. It took us four long and miserable days to arrive back in Massachusetts.

4

Believing in Myself Against the Odds

Finally, we arrived back in Massachusetts. Robert and I had a total of $225 between us. The three of us spent our first night with Robert's best friend, James. We owned no furniture, had no prospect of renting an apartment, we had no jobs, and no childcare for Angela. The next day, Robert and I went about attempting to find an inexpensive furnished apartment that was close to a subway station. We were fortunate on the second day after arrival back in Massachusetts. We found a two-bedroom apartment on Walnut Street in Roxbury. The apartment was not in the best of neighborhood. But I remember how Robert had promised me that he would always do everything possible to protect me from harm. Therefore, I put all of my concerns aside.

The next day, Robert went back to Auto City and was hired on the spot. I, on the other hand, went to Firemen's Fund Insurance Company and applied for a job. Prior to leaving Los Angeles, I had asked my supervisor for a letter of recommendation. She willingly had given me a letter of recommendation in a sealed envelope. During my interview, I handed my letter of recommendation to the interviewer.

After reading it, he said, "So, you are anti-social, according to this letter." I was baffled, stunned, and confused. I was lost for words. So, I just sat there speechless and dumbfounded. I did not know what to say or how to respond. Of course, I did not get a job there. I left and went to my former place of employment, which was Kemper Insurance Company, and was hired immediately.

I went and made arrangements for Angela to enter preschool in September. I had been given a lead by a girlfriend about an excellent private preschool and kindergarten program located close to our apartment in Roxbury. The owner of this private school was willing to provide childcare while I worked. I began working the following day. Once we were working, letters from Summerville Furniture Store's collection agency were sent to us requesting payment in full for our furniture Shirley had moved into her apartment and had agreed to pay the monthly payments until the account was paid in full.

To our amazement, neither she nor husband ever made one payment to Summerville Furniture Store. So for over a year, Summerville Furniture had not received any payments. Summerville Furniture Store was unaware of the verbal agreement between Shirley and me. Therefore, Robert and I were still responsible for this outstanding bill, and we arranged to pay monthly payments until the account was paid off. I never mentioned this predicament to Shirley or Larry, although we interacted with them for many years after returning to Massachusetts. I learned a valuable lesson from this incident and that was to get things in writing and notarized when necessary.

After Robert and I had earned a couple of paychecks, we went shopping for furniture, put it on lay-a-way, and began to save money to purchase a new car. We had decided that we would move to a better apartment in a better and safer neighborhood within one year and make a down payment for a new car. I liked the fact that our apartment was located only a few blocks from the subway station and the laundromat was nearby, too. The neighborhood was very busy and noisy. There were people out walking constantly and children played outside frequently as the parents watched them from their balconies. In this regard, I was very pleased that our apartment was not isolated and on a side street. As a result, I felt even safer.

Unfortunately, families of mice invaded our furnished apartment after a couple of months. I have already revealed that I was afraid of snakes. Well, I was afraid of mice and rats, too. And our apartment became a nightmare for Angela and me. We were afraid to be in the apartment when Robert was not there, and I was no comfort to Angela. I could not conceal my fear from her. Even after many years have passed, I still get goose bumps whenever I remember living in that apartment.

After about six months, I managed to get a better paying job at Blue Cross-Blue Shield Insurance Company. During this time, my sister Cassie had begun taking refresher courses at Odwin Health Careers, which was located about a mile from my apartment in Roxbury. She told me about this program and that it was free. The purpose of Odwin was to prepare individuals for college and to be successful while attending college. Immediately, I went and inquired about this college preparation program. I was evaluated on my current level of knowledge in English and math. I was accepted and began attending evening classes in English and math. When Cassie called me, I told her that I have been accepted into the Odwin program. She was just as thrilled for me as I was.

I attended Odwin two evenings each week. My instructors were very pleased with my progress, dedication, and enthusiasm and suggested that I attend classes more frequently, so that I could enter college in September. I thought about this for a few days. Then I went to work and gave Blue Cross-Blue Shield a two-week notice. After I had left my job, I immediately began taking day classes in English and math, and I enrolled in an inorganic chemistry class at a local prep school, because Odwin did not offer refresher classes in inorganic chemistry. My English instructor encouraged me to decide on a career path. I knew that I still wanted to become a doctor, but my life had taken a totally different direction than I ever imagined. I told my English instructor that I would like to become a dentist at some point in the future.

I honestly believe that it does not matter where I started out, but what matters is where I end up. It had been nearly seven years after I had graduated from high school, and I still had not attended college as I had originally planned. So, I entered Forsyth School for Dental

Hygienists in Boston in 1972, because I was unsure if I had the stamina to endure all those long years of study required to become a dentist. I reasoned that if I did not make it through dental school, at least I had acquired skills to earn an adequate income on a regular basis by becoming a dental hygienist. Robert and I moved to a beautiful apartment in a better and safer neighborhood in Mattapan with our brand new furniture. Angela had her own beautiful and spacious room. She was becoming more beautiful, brilliant, and happier and was growing like a weed. I was so very proud of her and very grateful that I was her mother.

I enjoyed attending classes at Forsyth. It did not matter to me that Forsyth was a two-year school. What mattered was that, finally, I could earn a living wage as a dental hygienist as I pursued my educational goals. All of my classes were interesting, and I was very excited about learning new concepts and facts each day. I had always enjoyed extra reading since middle school, so I thirsted to learn new knowledge. The dental hygiene students took several classes with Northeastern University students. Whenever I attended classes on the Northeastern campus, there were over 300 students in each class, whereas the dental hygiene classes held on the Forsyth campus had a little more than 100. To me, it did not matter the class size; I thrived in all of them. Years later I learned a valuable lesson that class sizes do matter. When I needed a recommendation from my former human anatomy and physiology professor, to my surprise, he did not remember me, and I remembered him as if it was yesterday. He instructed me to write what I wanted him to include in the recommendation, and he would have it typed and sent directly to the appropriate dental schools I was applying to. I did as he asked, and he kept his promise.

I could barely contain my excitement of finally attending college. I was never late for any of my classes. And for once in my lifetime, I was able to purchase every textbook required, because I had been awarded a partial scholarship by Forsyth and grants from the federal government. I was used to reading in my spare time for relaxation and fun. Attending Forsyth meant that I would be reading and acquiring new information that would benefit me for my present and my future. I heard some of my classmates complaining about our professors assigning too much reading assignments. I never complained out loud or silently, because I was thoroughly enjoying attending Forsyth and everything that went with it.

My core dental hygiene courses consisted of human anatomy and physiology, dental anatomy, and dental hygiene. These were the courses I excelled in. All of them required lots of hours of reading and studying. I found out that courses that required creative writing were very challenging for me. I remember this one creative writing assignment that required lots of my time just to decide on a topic. I pondered and pondered but without any success. I went to the Isabella Stewart Gardner Museum located a short distance from Forsyth in hopes of discovering a painting that would stimulate my creative senses and touch my inmost being, so that I could write a brilliant creative writing paper.

I chose a painting of a woman with the appearance of a ghost, or the way I imagine a vampire would look like. I spent multiple hours writing this two-page typed paper. I submitted my creative writing paper on time. A week later, I discovered that I had received a B for the grade. I was very disappointed because I was getting A's in all of my core courses. At the time, I did not realize that this would most likely become the norm for me in all of my courses, except for the science and math ones.

Another reason I was enjoying attending Forsyth was because my wardrobe was not an issue, since every day was dress down day. Therefore, I wore jeans and comfortable shoes every day with ease. On the days I was in the dental hygiene clinic learning the proper way to use the dental instruments, I wore a long white lab coats over our jeans. Later, when I actually was treating patients, I wore a white uniform and white cap, which were similar to those worn by registered nurses.

During my first year at Forsyth, I was awarded the Isabelle Kendrick's award for excellence in dental hygiene. It was up to the clinical instructors to vote for a first year student, and I had received the most votes. I was simultaneously humbled and honored. I was rejuvenated and felt that I could accomplish anything I made up my mind to do, as long as I was willing to work hard for it and earn it honestly.

Before completing my first year at Forsyth, our landlords experienced marital problems and separated. Robert and I were told that their multi-family house was being put on the market to be sold. We were advised that it would be best for us to find another apartment as soon as possible. With such short notice, we found an apartment in Mattapan on a side street between Blue Hill Avenue and Norfolk Street. The apartment was not what we wanted, but we needed a place to move into quickly. I did not feel safe living on Hosmer Street, because there were several adults that just loitered on Hosmer Street all time of day and night.

The summer after completing my first year at Forsyth, I was selected to participate in a collaborative ten-week program sponsored by Forsyth and Tufts University School of Dental Medicine (TUSDM). I believed this would provide opportunities for me to work with dental students, ask many questions about the dental program, and meet some dental professors. I took advantage of this opportunity.

The dental students told me that they were in a three-year undergraduate program at TUSDM, which meant that they did not have summers off from school. Many of them said that they planned on applying to postgraduate programs, so that they would become specialists in the dental professions, such as periodontists, endodontists, orthodontists, prosthodontists, and oral surgeons. These individual post-graduate programs required anywhere from two to six years of additional training. I desired to become either a periodontist or orthodontist. But I had to complete the undergraduate dental program first. Because I was already older than the majority of the first year dental students. I was very interested in applying to TUSDM's three-year program in the near future.

But after a month in the program, Robert's mom died, and we had to make arrangements to attend her home going celebration and funeral in Rosedale, Mississippi. Robert and I had recently purchased our first car a month earlier. It was a brand new Mercury Cougar. It had taken us 16 months to save for it, because we wanted to have a large down payment, so that our monthly payments would fit our monthly household expenses. It took us over 30 hours of driving to reach Rosedale, Mississippi. The three of us were totally exhausted upon our arrival there. But there was no time allowed for us to recover from our long trip.

As we attended Robert's mom's home going celebration and funeral, Robert was overcome with grief and sadness. Robert took his mom's death very hard. Watching Robert grieve was almost unbearable, and I did all I could to help him through his grief but to no avail. The drive back home to Massachusetts was very difficult for the three of us. We were all very exhausted from the drive to Mississippi because it had taken us 30 hours to drive there; the home going and funeral was the next day, and we had to start our return trip to Massachusetts the very next day. Robert did all of the driving to and from Mississippi, because I had recently gotten my driver's license. And neither of us felt comfortable with my driving on interstate highways.

After arriving back home, Angela and I adjusted back to normal. But Robert continued to grieve and became very depressed. Although I don't have any proof and Robert has never actually verbalized this, I believe Robert has always been closer to his mom than his daddy. Reflecting back to our conversations, Robert's facial expressions would soften and his voice would become gentler whenever he talked about his mom. I recognized these changes because several people had told me the same thing whenever I talked about Daddy. I felt that I had to do something to help Robert through this phase of his life, and it would take a major undertaken on my part. I was unsure if I could endure another major undertaken, especially if it would be a life changing one.

As I was pondering about Robert's current state of mind, I decided to make an appointment with my gynecologist/obstetrics, Dr. Barrera. During my appointment, I told him that I wanted to become pregnant, but I had been taking birth control faithfully for over six years. As a result, I was concerned about the possibility that I could have three or more babies at one time. Dr. Barrera was unsure whether I was sane right then or at least thinking straight. In the past and during every appointment, I had told Dr. Barrera to make sure I am not pregnant. If I were pregnant, he should flush it out before I left his office. Believe it or not, I had been very serious. This was just how much I did not want another baby then. After much discussion between us, Dr. Barrera advised me to be very careful for three months, and on the fourth month, I could let my guard down and let nature take its course. Without Robert's knowledge of my plans, I made myself inaccessible when I was ovulating and/or in doubt. Robert would say to me frequently that he had waited for me to come to bed. I would say to him that I was very sorry, but I had a lot of reading to do or I was studying for exams.

Once the three months were over, I made myself very accessible to Robert. Two weeks after missing my period, I went to see Dr. Barrera and was told that I was definitely pregnant and expect to give birth around June 17th the following year. I told Angela my good news and not to tell Daddy until we were having dessert that evening.

Well, as soon as Robert opened the front door, Angela ran to him and said, "Daddy, Daddy, mommy is having a baby!" He looked at me as if it he could not believe it but wanted to. After a few seconds, Robert asked me if this was true. I smiled and told him we were pregnant and to expect a baby boy or baby girl around June 17th. Robert's entire demeanor changed. He behaved as if he had swallowed a golden egg. He was so excited that he could barely contain himself and said, "God took his mama but is giving him a son." I prayed and hoped our baby would be a boy, although Angela wanted a baby sister.

Robert decided that our son deserved an African name, I, in turn, had decided that our son would be named Robert Jr. or our daughter would be named Roberta, since this was going to be my last pregnancy. From the onset, I had pregnancy sickness each and every day and throughout each day. I kept saltine crackers on the nightstand, so that I could eat a couple of them without lifting my head from my pillow. The crackers settled my stomach just enough so that I could bathe, dress, and attend my classes at Forsyth. Actually, attending classes and clinic were very helpful, because I was too busy to constantly concentrate on my pregnancy sickness during the day.

While I was in my third trimester, I received a phone call from Carrie that my maternal grandmother had died. This was on a Saturday afternoon. Robert was at work. I drove over to see my sister, Nellie and told her that our maternal grandmother had just died. I could have called her, but I did not want to tell her this news over the phone, and she lived only a few streets from me in Mattapan. Besides, we would be face to face and be able to hold and comfort each other. I was only gone from my apartment for less than two hours. When I returned home, the apartment was in total disarray. Someone had come into the apartment and stolen everything they felt was of value that could be taken in a short time. Even Angela's piggy bank was stolen. The thief or thieves had searched all of the drawers in the bedrooms and left them opened with some of the items on the floors.

Robert called the landlord, who lived in Maynard, Massachusetts, after arriving home from work and learning what had just happened. Robert explained that something had to be done immediately to secure the apartment for the safety of us all. The thief or thieves had damaged the front door of the apartment. The landlord showed up with a carpenter and the front door was repaired. We informed the landlord that we would be leaving first thing Monday morning driving to Alabama for my maternal grandmother's funeral and would he check on our apartment or have someone check on our apartment regularly while we were away. The landlord gave his promise that he would.

As soon as we returned from attending my maternal grandmother's funeral, we looked for another apartment outside of the metropolitan Boston area. We searched for an apartment in the Brockton area and chose one at Chateau Westgate, which was on Oak Street. It was a basement with the windows at ground level. The rental agency informed us that couples with very young children were not permitted to live above anyone. Since Robert and I were having a baby within a few months, we agreed to rent this basement apartment. One of the advantages of living in a basement apartment was that the washer and dryer were located directly down the corridor on the same floor.

No two pregnancies are alike, especially for me. With Angela, I lost weight and only gained a total of 14 pounds during pregnancy. With this second pregnancy, I was gaining weight rapidly. I experienced pregnancy sickness every day, and all the healthy foods made me feel even worse. So, I ate enormous amounts of unhealthy foods and very few healthy foods.

My second year was not enjoyable to me because of my daily pregnancy sickness. My classmates sympathized with me and did everything they could to help me out. They even brought different types of foods to school in hopes that I would be able to eat them. I was very grateful to them all. Somehow, I managed to complete all of my classes and passed all of my final exams and my clinical licensing exam on time. I said at the time that it was my pure will power that I finished on time. My graduation was scheduled close to my due date. I was so uncomfortable and big that I decided that I would not attend it. My family and I moved to Brockton in April 1974.

Baby Junior was born a week late on June 22nd and weighed seven pounds and four ounces. When Robert saw his baby boy for the first time, he forgot all about that special African name he had chosen and asked me if Bobby was all right, because he appeared to be very small. I smiled and said, yes, Bobby is just fine, and we would fatten him up a bit once he's home. Also, I knew the name I had chosen would be realized, although I had never shared my thoughts and feelings with Robert. Some things did not need to be discussed, and the name of our son was one of them. I felt certain that once Robert took one look at his new son that he could not resist naming him after himself. And it came to pass.

Unfortunately, I was 30 pounds heavier after giving birth to Bobby. Robert asked, "Which outfit should I bring you to wear home?" I quickly told him that I did want him to bring me an outfit because I would be wearing the same outfit I wore to the hospital. I thought to myself that Robert must have been joking; there was no way I could fit into any of my clothes.

I spent the next eight weeks dieting to lose the 30 extra pounds I had gained. Cassie had told me about a high protein diet; a person would eat only meats while on this diet. I had never heard of this diet, and besides, I never had gained more than six pounds in excess with my first pregnancy. Having to lose 30 pounds felt almost unattainable to me. I was desperate, and so I tried this high protein diet.

After being on this high protein diet a couple of days, I became aware of a repugnant odor and I thought this terrible odor was coming from Bobby. I thought there was something seriously wrong with my baby. So, I quickly called Robert to come home because there was a terrible odor coming from our baby son. It would take Robert over an hour to arrive home. In the meantime, I discovered that the terrible odor was from my bad breath. The chicken I was eating was being broken down to ketones in my body and gave off this awful odor that I had never smelled before in my life. By the time Robert arrived home, I very calmly told him that the odor was coming from my bad breath caused by the high protein diet I was on to lose weight. Robert said nothing and just shook his head. After checking out Bobby for himself, Robert went back to work. I believed that Robert would be telling our immediate families about the time I had him rush home from work, because I thought Bobby smelled bad. I was correct.

During the summer of 1974, I continued dieting and lost 30 pounds. It was not an easy feat. As a matter of fact, it took me eight weeks to lose the 30 pounds, and I was miserable the entire time. I refused to shop for bigger sizes of clothes. I was used to drinking plenty of water each day. As a matter of fact, water was my favorite beverage. In Alabama, drinking water was always free. But when I was on this high protein diet, I had to drink much more water and drink it more frequently in order to keep my halitosis at a minimum.

During that same summer, the apartment complex where we lived in Brockton had its own swimming pool and had hired a lifeguard. The lifeguard gave swimming lessons to anyone who wanted them before the pool opened. I enrolled Angela to take swimming lessons every day at 9:00 AM five days a week. I would watch Angela from my front apartment window as she took swimming lessons. In no time at all, Angela was swimming without any assistance. It was as if Angela was related to fish. Other than dieting, I enjoyed being home with Angela and Bobby.

As the summer months passed, I decided that I would like to go back to work in September. So, I called Forsyth and inquired about a teaching job. I scheduled an interview with Dean of Forsyth and her assistant Dean. They both knew me very well and hired me on the spot. So, I began teaching in September as a full-time dental hygiene instructor.

Then, I enrolled at Northeastern University as a full-time student majoring in Health Science toward a bachelor degree. I was enjoying my new baby, my new job, and my course load at Northeastern University. Overall, I was overburdened with responsibilities. Yet I was determined to persevere through it all. My first year of teaching was relatively easy for me, because I was in the clinic the majority of the time.

I discovered that I was very good at teaching others. It never dawned on me to become a teacher before, and the reason I wanted to teach was two-fold. First, it meant that Forsyth provided vouchers to all full-time instructors that would pay for two courses each semester. Second, I was very good at scaling teeth. I had confidence in my clinical skills as a dental hygienist, because my previous professors had affirmed this in my first year as a dental hygiene student. They had voted me to win the Isabelle Kendrick's award for being the student who had demonstrated excellent overall dental hygiene skills.

My second year of teaching became very challenging, mainly because all clinical instructors were assigned additional teaching responsibilities outside of clinic. One of my colleagues and I were given the responsibilities to teach all first and second year didactic courses, which included formulating all examinations, proctoring them, and grading them all. In addition, I was assigned to manage the second year students' externship assignments by visiting each preceptor site at least once per semester and to arrange and host an annual meeting with them all at Forsyth.

I remember taking up to ten courses some semesters in order to complete all the course requirements for my Bachelor degree in Health Science. If I had not, I would have to wait an entire year for the courses that I needed to be offered again. My life was still hard, but still, it was never as hard as it had been while I lived in Alabama. Besides, I was working toward fulfilling my long held goal of becoming a doctor.

As I was struggling to fulfill my obligations, I shared my aspirations of becoming a dentist with daddy, my father-in-law, and Dr. Niosi. Dr. Niosi was a general dentist and worked a couple days a week in the dental clinic at Boston City Hospital. I had met him when I had taken some of my dental hygiene students to the dental clinic at Boston City Hospital.

Believe it or not, Daddy, my father-in-law, and, Dr. Niosi told me practically the same thing. Daddy and my father-in-law told me that it was too late for me to become a dentist and time had passed me by. Now, my obligations were to my family. Dr. Niosi told me that I did not need to become a dentist, since I was a dental hygienist. I did not respond to any of their comments, and I continued to think my own thoughts.

As I continued my hectic schedule, Robert and I rarely spent time together. The major problem was that Robert and I had totally different schedules, and we had only one car. Every morning, Robert and I would leave home at 4:30 AM to drive to his job in East Boston.

Then I would drive the car home. Once home, I would dress and feed the children. Angela would wait inside the apartment until she heard the school bus was coming and then go out and board it. Then I would leave and drive Bobby to the childcare provider.

Every morning after dropping Bobby off at the childcare provider, I would drive to Forsyth. Every afternoon after work, Robert would take the trolley to Forsyth for the car, drive to the childcare provider, and pick up Bobby and then drive home. Angela would already be home doing her homework and then watching television. Robert would serve them their dinner and put them to bed at the appropriate time. Angela and Bobby were left alone in the apartment while Robert drove into Boston to Northeastern to pick me up after my last class. The children were usually asleep before Robert left. On a few occasions, Robert had the children in the car with him. They would be sound asleep in the car when Robert arrived to pick me up at 9:00 PM. When we arrived back home around 9:45 PM, Robert and I carried Angela and Bobby into the apartment and put them to bed.

Angela was thriving and growing up faster than I was prepared for, and Bobby was thriving, too. When Bobby was nine-months-old, Robert and I began to have childcare problems. The childcare provider would allow Bobby to wear soiled diapers for long periods of time. At first, I gave her the benefit of doubt. But when I changed Bobby's diaper on that particular day, I had to soak him the bathtub in order to remove all of the hardened feces from his bottom. As soon as Robert arrived home, I told him about the situation. We both were extremely upset. I called my sister Carrie, who lived in Alabama, and asked her if she would be willing to fly to Massachusetts and take Bobby back with her on the same weekend. She agreed immediately after hearing about Robert and my childcare problem. I proceeded to make the airline reservations for Carrie.

Robert and I sent money to Carrie every month to cover Bobby's expenses and extra money, so that Carrie would have money to spend as she desired. Carrie and Mack would tell Robert and me that having Bobby in their home was such a great joy. We were unsure if their children felt the same way. Bobby stayed in Alabama until he was two-years-and-nine-months-old.

With Bobby staying with Carrie and Mack, I knew he was being taken care of properly. However, I wished I could have figured out a better way, so that I could have kept him with me. Although the responsibility of having but one child at home made things easier for me,

I still missed my baby terribly. But every time I thought about Bobby with dried feces on his body and wearing wet soggy diapers for long periods of time, it reassured me that he was better off just where he was. And that was in Alabama with Carrie and Mack.

I knew Bobby was approaching the age that certified childcare providers would accept him to their programs. I began interviewing different ones, and I settled on a certified childcare provider who had established her childcare services in her home. It was operated by Mrs. Burdett and was located in Dorchester. Mrs. Burdett was a grandmother and old enough to be my mother. After our interview, I chose her program and enrolled Bobby.

Then I flew to Alabama for my son and returned the same weekend. On my return trip home, Bobby cried all the way. He thought I was actually separating him from his mommy and daddy and cried out for them all the way back to Massachusetts and for days after we had returned.

I was thrilled that Bobby was finally home, although it took him some time to adjust to Robert and me. Bobby would stay close to Angela and followed her throughout the apartment. Angela was very pleased to have Bobby back home, and she never fully understood why he was sent away in the first place. Robert and I had explained the reasons why we had sent Bobby to Alabama to Angela on several occasions. But Angela still felt that since Bobby was her brother, no one had the right to separate the two of them from each other. This was just one of those situations that life had presented us with and all four of us had gotten through it the best we could.

After graduating from Northeastern University in 1976, I scheduled an interview with Admissions at Tufts University School of Dental Medicine (TUSDM). I was informed that I needed to take additional science courses, because some of the sciences courses I had taken were not advanced enough to prepare me for success in dental school. I thanked the admissions person, left, and immediately went to Northeastern and applied for a special student status. I then enrolled in biology, physics, and organic chemistry.

In the fall of 1977, I applied to TUSDM and requested to be considered for early admission. I was scheduled for an interview. On the day of the interview, I was so nervous that I could not drink or eat anything. I remember that Dr. Patricia Brown interviewed me. I had seen her a few years back while I was a student at Forsyth, and I knew Dr. Brown was an orthodontist. Dr. Brown encouraged me to relax. She had a beautiful wide smile on her face as I looked directly at her. I could feel that my breathing was becoming less rapid and my hands were beginning to stop sweating. Evidently, I passed the interview because I received an early acceptance letter a couple weeks later to the incoming class of DMD 1981. This was a three-year program, which meant I would not have any summer breaks from school. I was not working at this time.

I had approximately six months before I entered dental school on my hands because I had completed all of the advance sciences courses, which were scheduled during the day. So, I decided to find a night job that I could leave without feeling guilty about when it was time to start dental school. I was hired as a nurse's aide at Newton-Wellesley Hospital. I lasted one night. There was one elderly patient who soiled his clothes and bed at least four times during my first night. My work schedule was from 11:00 PM to 7:00 AM. I called Robert during my break and explained this disgusting situation I had gotten myself in.

He said, "Margaret, you don't have to work at that job. Just leave." Well, I stayed until I my shift ended, left, and never looked backed. I did not realize at the time that these upcoming months would be the last relatively sane ones for me until I graduated from dental school.

I did my best to prepare Robert, Angela, Bobby, immediate family members, and close friends to expect very little from me while I was attending dental school. The discussions I had with my family dentist and other dentists had told me to prepare myself for the most demanding endeavor I could ever imagine. And so I attempted to prepare everyone who mattered to me. I planned and held my last dinner party during those few months and explained to my family and friends that for the next three years, the Howards would only accept invitations to family gatherings and not host them. Everyone seemed to understand and accepted the fact that I would be too involved with dental school.

While waiting to begin attending TUSDM, I applied for the National Health Service Corp (NHSC) scholarship to pay for my dental education. This scholarship would pay my tuition, books, fees, cost of dental instruments, and provide me with a monthly stipend. I was counting on this scholarship to finance my dental education, because Robert and my savings were inadequate to cover the three years. We had enough money saved to cover everything for the first year, except the cost of my dental instruments. If I were awarded the NHSC scholarship, the Navy would classify me as a lieutenant in the active reserve branch of the Navy. And upon graduating from TUSDM, I would repay this debt by working in a community health center in an underserved and under-represented population with the approval of the NHSC.

Finally, it was time for me to start dental school. On my first day at TUSDM, I was very excited and nervous. As it turned out, I was not alone. I was the first college graduate in my immediately family and the first future dental medical doctor as well. There were many first year dental students who were the first in their families to graduate from college and the first future dental medical doctors among my classmates. I felt right at home and knew it was meant for me to attend TUSDM all along. I was grateful, thrilled, and very pleased with my accomplishments thus far. I had worked very hard over the last several years; I had made sacrifices that only I could fully understand. And there was still much work for me complete, but I felt and believed that I would measure up to those challenges.

As it turned out, my first year at TUSDM almost got the best of me. I had never imagined that an educational program could be so difficult. Reflecting back on my experiences at Northeastern University and comparing those challenges with the challenges I was facing now was like comparing day and night. I cried every night as I drove home. One night I was so distraught that I was speeding on Route 24 South and a state police officer pulled me over. When he took one look at me, he became less stern and official, because I was crying hysterically with mascara running down my face. All he said to me was calm down and drive safely. The state police officer did not even give me a ticket or warning. After a few minutes, I continued driving home.

Another factor that made dental school a challenge for me was that it placed a heavy financial burden on Robert and me, because I did not receive the NHSC scholarship I had applied for. Cassie came to my rescue and paid for all of my dental instruments and supplies, and they were very expensive.

I was very disappointed in not receiving the scholarship. So, I wrote President Jimmy Carter a letter explaining that I was one of 18 children and aspiring to become a dentist, so that I could provide comprehensive dental care to the underserviced population in an underrepresented community. And I had not received the NHSC scholarship, which I had hoped to receive. I later received a very thoughtful and kind letter from President Carter, advising me to reapply for the scholarship.

I did as he advised and received the scholarship for the next two years, along with a monthly stipend. Our financial woes had ended. Yet I was still struggling with my time management, and I began to consider that maybe I could go from being high to low maintenance of myself. As a result, I made a major decision that I would regret for the rest of my life.

I had stopped straightening my hair many years earlier and was wearing it in an afro. Reserving the time for my haircare had never been an issue before I entered dental school. Up until this point in time, I had never experienced any difficulties in managing my hair, and I was very pleased with the results, although it consumed an ample amount of my personal time. By October, I felt that there were not enough hours in the day for me to keep up with my classes and fulfill family obligations, and I needed to figure ways to spend less time on my personal needs without neglecting myself. Well, I figured that if I had a perm in my hair, this would free up at least a few hours each week. I consented to having a perm, so that I could devote those few hours I had saved to studying. As it turned out, the advantages were far less than the disadvantages. The perm damaged my hair and made it very weak and stringy.

Now it took more time than previously to manage my haircare. I learned a valuable lesson from this experience and that was chemical treatments for my hair was a mistake, although the daily maintenance of hair required less time, the results were devastating to my scalp and hair. It would take a couple of years for my scalp and hair to fully recover. Also, I discovered that looks can be deceiving. The grass is not always greener in someone else's yard. In other words, what worked for others does not mean it would work for me. Then I remembered an incident that had occurred during my senior year in high school. Mrs. McLoyd was the mother-in-law of my former fifth grade teacher. She had advised me to never put a perm in my hair, because I had thick black hair, and a perm would damage it. I had given my promise. Now I had broken my promise, and I was suffering the consequences.

Although I had become friendly with several of the female and male dental students over the last three months, I discovered that some of them had copies of old dental exams that I was never privy to. Since I had no clue where those old exams originated from, I could not do anything about it. Therefore, I struggled in silence. In addition, I felt that the preclinical professors spent more time with certain students than others, espccially the single female ones. I was afraid to share my opinion concerning this matter with anyone connected with TUSDM. But I made a promise to myself that I would willingly share my knowledge, wisdom, experiences, expertise, and professional skills with others. And I would be inclusive rather than exclusive in my sharing.

As my Christmas break was approaching, Robert, Angela, and Bobby were looking forward to our vacation. I, on the other hand, was not thinking about any kind of vacation, except using the week off from school to catch up on my assigned readings. But, Robert insisted that I needed to help him with the plans. This additional task was too much for me to handle. The demands of dental school were overwhelming. I tried to explain this to Robert, but he was not receptive. Instead, Robert became adamant and continued to insist on my input.

So, one day, I responded sharply to him and said, "Robert, I don't care where we go. Just remember to tell me whether it will be warm or cold."

At one point during my first year at TUSDM, I felt as if I were having a complete nervous breakdown. I went to see a therapist and discussed my problems with her. After my appointment, I became paranoid and thought there was a possibility that she would tell someone at TUSDM and

I would be expelled. Finally, I mustered up enough courage and met with one of my older professors. His name was Dr. Wetz. After listening to me, he assured me that I was doing just fine in school. Dr. Wetz explained to me that when very intelligent dental students are in the same class, some are placed in the middle. I placed in the middle, and being in the middle is not a bad thing. He continued by saying that he had complete confidence in me that I would never fail any exams; I would do very well providing dental services to my assigned patients, and I would pass my dental licensing exam with flying colors. I thanked him and left his office. I held on to Dr. Wetz's every encouraging word as if my life depended on them and considered them as my lifeline to success. My struggles continued in school and at home, but I persevered.

I was getting an average of three hours of sleep each night during the week. My day would begin at 2:30 AM, so that I could read and study for four hours. I had to make sure Angela and Bobby were dressed and fed before I left each morning. It took me at least an hour to arrive on time to my 8:00 AM class. At the end of each day, I went to the preclinical laboratory and practiced prepping the different categories of preparations for amalgam and crown restorations. Each night, I would arrive home around 11:00 PM and was in bed by 11:30 PM. Nevertheless, I wanted to be become a dentist so badly that I was determined not to give in or give up.

As it turned out, Dr. Wetz had been correct. I passed all of my exams and successfully completed my first year. I thought to myself, one down and two more to go. I had a one week vacation before beginning my second year of dental school. Robert, Angela, Robert Jr. and I spent time with family members in Alabama and Mississippi. That vacation week passed rapidly, and before I knew it, it was over. I was very exhausted from the hectic week of visiting our families living out of state. But there was nothing I could do about it, except just go with it. By the way, at some point over the previous year, Bobby had insisted that he should be called Robert because he was learning to spell and print his given first name. I explained to him that if I called him Robert and his dad Robert, this would be confusing for all of us. We reached a compromise on the matter, and Bobby became Robert Jr. from then on.

As my dental education and training progressed, my second year of dental school was less stressful. I discovered that all of my classmates were experiencing their own challenges, too. For instance, one of the smartest academic dental students in my class had a complete nervous breakdown and had to take a leave of absence from school. This information was revealed to me the first week of my second year. Collectively, we chose to associate with only dental students because only dental students understood what dental students were going through. We called it the dental crazies. I know Robert and my non-dental friends did not comprehend the challenges I faced as a dental student. I did not have time or energy to explain everything to them. I told Robert that I was married to TUSDM's requirements, and he had to be the mom and dad for our children. And that once I graduated, I would resume my parenting responsibilities.

During the first month of my second year at TUSDM, I entered the undergraduate clinic and began treating patients. I felt very comfortable taking patients' comprehensive health histories, taking their blood pressure readings, completing oral examinations – including all of required dental and periodontal charting – reviewing and interpreting full mouth radiographs, evaluating patients' plaque-free scores, teaching patients proper oral hygiene, and performing oral prophylaxes, and subgingival scaling. The reasons I was very comfortable and very proficient in all of the above mentioned procedures was because they were the same ones I had been taught and trained in while I attended Forsyth. I was experienced in dealing with patients' tongues, cheeks, saliva, and keeping their mouths opened.

The dental students who were not dental hygienists did not adjust as well as I did in the undergraduate clinic. When they were struggling to adjust to patients' tongues, cheeks, saliva, and keeping mouths opened, I was formulating and completing the patients' treatment plans and completing the periodontal phase one portion of assigned dental patients' dental treatment.

Although I did extremely well providing dental treatment to patients with simple gingivitis and slight to moderate periodontal disease, I struggled to obtain clearance for the dental patients to proceed to the restorative portion of their treatment whenever they were diagnoscd with severe periodontal disease. It was not because I could not thoroughly perform the deep subgingival scaling treatment; I struggled to obtain clearance because of the patient's non-compliance in maintaining good to excellent oral hygiene and failing to keep their scheduled appointments.

By the end of my second year, which was the end of my first year in the undergraduate clinic providing direct dental care to patients, I was behind in my clinical requirements. And my dental manager informed me on several occasions that if I kept this pace up, I would not graduate on time. I became very concerned about the possibility that I might have to extend my stay in dental school longer than I had anticipated. Besides, Robert, Angela, Robert Jr., and the NHSC were depending on me to graduate in June 1981.

I decided on a strategy to use on my assigned non-compliant patients to help me with my on time graduation. So, I hoped for the best. I promised each non-compliant patient a lobster dinner at their restaurant of choice, if they kept all of their future scheduled dental appointments with me. Believe it or not, this strategy worked successfully with many of them, and by the end of the summer of 1980, I was on schedule in meeting all of my clinical requirements needed to clear for graduation.

Because I was very shrewd when it came to selecting my five-week senior externship, I was assigned at the Veterans Administration Hospital (VAH) in the dental clinic, which was located on Huntington Avenue in Jamaica

Plain, Massachusetts. Because of the proximity of my five-week externship to TUSDM, I was permitted to treat the patients who needed gold inlays and onlays. As it turned out, one of TUSDM's clinical professors worked in the dental clinical at VAH. He was very helpful in teaching me how to take excellent rubber base impressions on edentulous patients and fabricating good to excellent fitting permanent complete dentures. At the end of my five week externship program, I had met the complete dentures requirement that was allowed from a preceptor of TUSDM. Now I only needed two more complete dentures, and my oral surgery rotation was scheduled as soon as my externship was completed.

On my first day in oral surgery rotation, I was fortunate to be assigned a patient in dental pain, needing all of his remaining teeth extracted. During this appointment, the patient was experiencing excruciating pain from a non-restorable broken-down tooth. After the oral surgery professor approved me to extract that tooth, the patient refused to be treated by me. The patient said that he wanted a white dental student to extract his tooth. Immediately, I informed my professor about the patient's request. My professor walked into the treatment room where the patient was sitting and informed him that he had two options: 1. Leave immediately and never return to TUSDM, or 2. Allow Margaret to extract the tooth. The patient chose to remain in the dental chair; I extracted the tooth and scheduled the patient for alginate impressions with me. This turned out to be the last set of dentures I needed in order to graduation on time.

During the time I was fabricating this patient's complete upper and lower dentures, he was diagnosed with advance lung cancer. By the time I was in the last few months of dental school, I was literally wheeling this patient to the undergraduate dental clinic for his final complete denture adjustments, so that I would receive full credit for my last required dentures. This patient was in the last stage of his life and spending his last days in Tufts University Medicine Center (TUSMC), and I was more concerned with receiving full credit for the upper and lower dentures. In hindsight I regret my behavior very much, although I was suffering from a chronic case of the dental crazies at that time.

As time passed, Robert became very miserable in our marriage, and I felt the same way. I pleaded with Robert not to make any rash decisions while I was in school because I was only going through the dental crazies. I assured him that the woman he had married would return to him normal, better, and stronger. He was there for our children, and I was there for TUSDM's requirements and this was the way we existed for at least two years, and we continued to be miserably married to each other.

Up until I started dental school, all of the parenting responsibilities had been mine. Now, since Robert had most of the parenting responsibilities, he did not adjust well to them. Robert did make sure the children were fed and bathe. But as far as cleaning up after the children and himself, he did absolutely nothing and left everything for me to do. Robert acted as if we had a maid coming in every day. I, on the other hand, was too tired to mention or complain about his neglect. I kept my dissatisfaction with his attitude and his neglect of the housework to myself and completed those household chores as fast as possible. I found myself writing down things I disliked about Robert's behavior and decided to address all of these matters once I graduated from dental school.

Eventually, I bought a black book just to record the things I disliked about Robert. Sometimes, I wondered to myself if Robert was keeping a record of all the things he disliked about me. Since we had both agreed not to discuss serious matters until I graduated, we remained miserably married and we honored our agreement.

In hindsight I realized that all of our so-called close friends were persons Robert had become friends with while I was busy working full-time and attending college full-time. The only close friends I had remained Cassie, Maxine, and Diane. If they were such close friends of Robert, I wondered where were they when Robert was experiencing difficulties being a father and mother to our children. None of his friends came forward to help him, although they assured him that it did not take anyone that much time to get through dental school. By the way, none of Robert's friends had ever attended dental school or knew anyone close to them who had attended dental school at the time. As a matter of fact, I was the first person they knew personally who was attending dental school.

I thoroughly enjoyed the patient/doctor relationship with my assigned patients. I was finally practicing dentistry – all phases of general dentistry. I had excellent clinical professors to guide, teach, and evaluate my progress along the way. It turned out that they were the same professors I had in preclinical laboratory. This was a good thing for me, because each one knew my clinical skill levels in all phases of general dentistry and could help me strengthen my weak ones and improve my strong ones. I passed all of my exams and was promoted to my third year.

Robert opened a used car dealership and auto body repair business in August 1980, which was during my senior year. Angela and Robert Jr. were growing up faster than I would like. Yet, they were typical normal and active children. Robert and I kept them busy so that they were not bored, since we were very busy working long hours each day. Our children were latch key children and were very responsible.

My senior year of dental school involved lunchtime seminars, primarily, and treating patients from 9:00 AM to 12:00 noon and from 1:00 PM to 4:00 PM. I spent all of my extra time in the dental lab pouring up alginate and final impressions, waxing up crowns, bridges, fabricating partial dentures and complete dentures, and other laboratory tasks from 6:00 PM until 11:00 PM four nights each week. I did not enjoy getting dirty in the lab, but I enjoyed the results of my hard work. Robert became my dental patient, along with Cassie and Maxine. Their dental needs were very helpful in meeting my dental requirements in restorative and prosthodontics. They always showed for their scheduled appointments and were never tardy for any of them.

I cleared from TUSDM two full months before my graduation date. I stopped by all of the departments and thanked those individuals who had assisted me doing my dental experiences at TUSDM. Some of them told me that I had been a model student. They said I always had a smile on my face and heard me speaking kind words to everyone. You see, I never cried at TUSDM during the entire three years. I always waited until I was in my car driving home. And my parents had taught me to keep my thoughts to myself whenever I did not have any kind words to say to others. I just practiced what I had been taught.

During those two months before I graduated, I spent time nurturing my scalp and follicles back to health, because the perm I had the first year of dental school caused my beautiful jet black and curly hair to break off. I promised myself that I would never consent to another perm. In addition, I felt freedom and relief to have completed my dental requirements in advance of my graduation, which was to be on Sunday, June 9, 1981. Slowly, I acclimated to being a loving wife to Robert and an accessible mother to our two children.

As I was waiting to graduate from dental school, Mama was diagnosed with breast cancer. Cassie was a first-year medical student at Rutgers Medical School in Piscataway, New Jersey and had learned the correct way to exam her breasts. She proceeded to teach Mama and all of her sisters how to correctly examine our breasts on a monthly basis. During Cassie's demonstration to Mama, she discovered a lump in Mama's left breast. Well, Cassie was not very concerned, and neither was I, because we believed in early detection and treatment. As it turned out, Mama was told by her physician that the cancer had metastasized; she agreed to an aggressive treatment of this cancer, which involved a mastectomy of her left breast. The prognosis was not good. Mama came through the treatment as well as could be expected. But her children did not.

None of the Williams' siblings were prepared for this dismal news, although we did our best to conceal our true feelings when we were with Mama and Daddy. Many of my siblings had not abandoned their faith in God, as I had done, and prayed to God for complete healing of Mama. Mama and Daddy were strong in their faith and believed that all of us would be all right, regardless of the outcome. I, too, prayed to God, although praying had become something I did whenever things were not going well for my family and me.

While Robert was at work and Angela and Robert Jr. were in school, I interviewed at different public health clinics in New England as far away as Stamford, Connecticut for a position. I was offered the opportunity to establish a community health center in Stamford, but I chose to work at Harvard Street Neighborhood Health Center (HSNHC) located on Blue Hill Avenue in Dorchester, Massachusetts. I discovered that Dr. Niosi was the Dental Director at HSNHC. I chose this location for three reasons. First, Robert and I would not have to relocate. Second, I would be providing comprehensive dental care to underserved and underrepresented populations. Third, I was familiar with the community because HSNHC was located across the street from Franklin Park.

My graduation from TUSDM was uneventful. Only Robert, Angela, and Robert Jr. attended my graduation because the rest of my family was busy helping Mama and Daddy. I flew home for four days to visit Mama as soon as I could after my graduation. I was of little help. But three of my sisters, Nellie, Carrie, and Burnestine provided 24-hour comprehensive care for them both since Daddy was completely blind from glaucoma during this time.

The NHSC finalized my appointment at HSNHC for two years. On my first day at HSNHC, a woman with a beautiful smile greeted me, and her name was Ruth. She was absolutely thrilled to have me working at HSNHC. Ruth was a very experienced dental assistant and readily put me at ease. I, on the other hand, was a nervous wreck.

Although I felt qualified as a general dentist, I knew I was very slow and it would take time for me to increase my speed and maintain quality in the dental care I would be providing my patients. Ruth assured me that I would do just fine. I took her at her word, and I was. On the other hand, the other women dental assistants were not very cooperative in making my workdays as pleasant as possibile. They would not readily clean my treatment rooms for the next scheduled patients, and they delayed cleaning the lab counters after I had poured up impressions and the like. Both dental assistants' demeanors were different with the male dentists. I regarded Ruth as my savior, and my two years at HSNHC were overall very rewarding. My speed increased tremendously; my confidence in my dental knowledge and skills were confirmed, and I felt that I finally realized my goal of being able to take care of myself regardless of what the future held.

I had two wonderful and experienced veteran dentists as mentors as I treated a wide array of patients with various degrees of challenging dental needs. TUSDM had prepared me very well in the prevention of dental diseases, diagnosing dental problems, formulating comprehensive treatment options, restoring dental health and function, and improving esthetics, whenever possible. But I was very poorly prepared to extract the different degrees of hopeless teeth. And I soon realized that I needed additional experience in extracting hopeless teeth. Therefore, I made arrangements to spend every Monday morning at the Boston City Hospital Dental Emergency Clinic where I would learn through observation, assisting oral surgeons with complex extractions, and extraction of hopeless teeth. My oral surgical skills greatly improved.

Although the two veteran dentists graciously shared their professional expertise with me, I was perplexed by Dr. Niosi's attitude toward me. One would think that he would have been pleased that I had become a general dentist, as I had planned years ago. Instead he never offered to help mentor me in any dental procedure during the entire two years I worked at HSNHC. Dr. Niosi had known me before I had become a dentist, whereas the two veteran dentists only met me when I began working at HSNHC. I felt very gratified that Dr. Niosi discovered that I had not allowed his comments about me not needing to become a dentist to influence me. Besides, I already knew that I was an excellent dental hygienist with or without his comments. Earlier on in life, I had learned that I only failed myself if I did not apply my best efforts in all endeavors I had committed to, and honest hard work should never be a deterrent in realizing my goals.

Yet, it would not have cost, Dr. Niosi, anything to extend his professional courtesy and expertise to me and helped me to become a better dentist. He had had two years of opportunities, and all I had received from him was criticism. I was so very grateful to have had two younger veteran dentists who generously shared their knowledge, experiences, and expertise in all phases of general dentary with me. As a result, I became a much better general dentist. And throughout my tenure at HSNHC, I demonstrated my gratitude to them with words of genuine praises and thanksgiving.

As time passed, Mama was still not doing well. She was never diagnosed as being cancer-free. Cassie concentrated on instructing Mama in holistic remedies while I concentrated on paying for Mama's medications. This was a perfect arrangement for Cassie and me because, Cassie was a medical student with limited finances, and I could afford to pay for Mama's medications.

5

The Valleys and the Mountain Tops

Although, the pressure and demands of dental school were in the past, Robert and I were still going through a rough time in our marriage. I had been out of dental school for over a year. It was now August 1982, and Mama was bedridden and required constant care. I flew home to Alabama to visit Mama and ask Daddy's permission to divorce, Robert. I even took the small black book with a record of the reasons I needed a divorce. Daddy reached and took the book from my hand. He reminded me of the conversation we had 14 years ago regarding my decision to marry Robert. Our conversation had centered around me not pursuing my goals and my unpreparedness for marriage. Daddy reminded me that he had given me 10 years to adjust to being married, and I had not indicated to him that Robert and I were experiencing any marital problems during those 10 years.

Since I had not consulted with Daddy during those ten years, he had been thanking God for Robert, his son-in-law, ever since. Daddy told me to go home and be the best wife possible. He advised me that once Robert and I had resolved each argument, let each one remain dead forever. And to remember that each future argument or disagreement would be a totally new issue that should be resolved as such. Well, I cried throughout our conversation. Daddy advised me to report back to him in about a year, and in the meantime, he would be praying for Robert and me.

The next day, I could barely put on my mascara because of my tears. Every time I thought about facing Robert caused me to cry more profusely. I cried all the way from the hotel in Dothan, Alabama to Dothan Airport. I cried all the way from Dothan Airport to Hartfield-Jackson International Airport in Atlanta, Georgia. And I cried all the way from Hartfield-Jackson International Airport to Boston Logan International Airport.

Back in the day, there was no such thing as waterproof mascaras. My faced appeared as if it was done up for a Halloween party. But I did not care. On all three flights, the flight attendants avoided me as if I had bubonic plague. My eyes were very swollen and very red from crying. I was torn between whether to be obedient to Daddy or ask Robert for a divorce upfront. I decided on an alternative approach.

After arriving in Massachusetts, I chose to move to Easton with our two children. I found an apartment for Robert in East Bridgewater and helped him shop for furniture. Robert had unlimited visitation rights with the children. I consulted a lawyer regarding a legal separation and potential divorce proceedings. I informed Robert that if he wanted our marriage reconciled, he would have to ask me out on dates, and there would be no sexual relationships during our dating. He could invite me to dinners at his apartment or restaurants. Robert agreed to this arrangement. During our time to together, we were very honest with each other and revealed everything we disliked about one another. Robert even told me that he had always hated the way I chewed gum.

Over the next two months, we covered every topic without any animosity toward each other. Afterward, we reached an agreement to reconcile our differences, to symbolically burn the past, and to move back in together. Robert said if he moved in, he would not be moving out, because he loved me and desired with all of his heart to remain married to me. I agreed with him and helped Robert move in to the beautiful apartment located in a beautiful and safe neighborhood my children and I had lived in for the last two months. We stayed there for about a year and then we bought our first house in December 1982.

As Robert and I recommitted ourselves to each other and our marriage, Mama died on October 31st, 1982 in bed while she slept. All of us took Mama's death very hard. Robert, Angela, Robert Jr. and I drove to Alabama to be with the family and attend Mama's home going celebration and funeral. This would be the first time I had to participate in any preparations required for a funeral. I had no idea what I should do or where to begin. Thankfully, Carrie and Daddy knew what needed to be accomplished, because all of the rest of my family was as clueless as I was. Because I had been raised attending church from birth, I was very familiar with death and eternal life for all believers in Jesus Christ after death. But when it came to Mama's death, this was totally a different prospective for me. I had never imagined that Mama would not live to be very old. And yet, Mama died at the age of 59. It was almost too much for any of the Williams' siblings to handle. But Daddy came through and provided strength for all of us. He became my physical rock.

During my two year tenure at HSNHC, I took advantage of the continuing education (CE) courses offered at the Bethesda Navy Hospital, Walter Reed. Although I was in the navy active reserves and never wore any navy uniforms, I had all of the rights and privileges as the active duty navy lieutenants. The active duty lieutenants behaved as gentlemen in my presence and invited me to dine with them in the evenings. All of them knew that I was in Bethesda, Maryland strictly for the CE courses. Sometimes, I would schedule enough CE courses for two weeks consecutively. All of the CE courses were free, and Bethesda Navy Hospital had some of the best trained and knowledgeable dentists facilitating the courses.

After taking a two week CE course in designing and fabricating cast partial dentures, my skills and confidence increase tremendously. On my return to HSNHC after my two week CE course on cast partial dentures, I was very proficient in designing all types of cast partial dentures for my dental patients.

During my second year at HSNHC, I began asking questions about how does one go about opening a dental practice. I wanted to know all of the details, including the advantages and disadvantages. I figured some of the advantages of owning my own dental practice were the potential of earning more money, and I would have control of my work schedule.

Since I was still considered an inexperienced dentist, I did not know many of my colleagues very well professionally, and they did not know me very well professionally. Although I asked tough questions about what I needed to know about establishing and operating a dental practice, I sensed that they were being evasive and keeping those important details to themselves. On the other hand, my two mentors at HSNHC had never owned their own dental practice and could not help me. Then, about six months into my second year, a part-time general dentist started working at HSNHS. I soon discovered that he established his dental practice in his house. He treated dental patients three days per week in his own dental office and three days per week at HSNHC. This newly employed dentist at HSNHC went as far as to recommend a dental supply company to contact and a bank to discuss my business plans with, if I decided on opening a dental practice. All of this occurred between us in a matter of a couple of months.

Although I do not recall the part-time dentist's name, I do clearly remember that he had been very generous in sharing his professional knowledge and wisdom with me. And we had met for the first time when he began working at HSNHC. Go figure. This dentist was my ram in the bush, which God had provided just for me.

Once I had fulfilled my obligation to the National Health Service Corp, I opened a solo dental office in a severely underserviced and underrepresented community in Roxbury, MA in August 1983. It was a beautiful dental practice. I had chosen earth tone colors with two treatment rooms, and each treatment room had its own x-ray machine. My office was located across the street from the Tobin Middle School and Pleasant Hill Baptist Church. I had chosen to locate my dental office in an underserviced and underrepresented community, thereby remaining loyal to my commitment of providing quality dental care to populations of people who normally had not received continuous dental care.

Previously, my office had been a physician's office, which provided two advantages for me. First, everyone living in the community-at-large was accustomed to having a doctor in the neighborhood. Second, the interior of the office required minimum alterations. This was very important because it reduced the bottom line costs for converting it into a dental office.

As I was determined to further my aspirations to the next level, I had overlooked one major aspect. I had not talked to God or asked the Holy Spirit for guidance in this business venture in advance. I do not recall ever praying to God and asking God's blessings at all. Years later the Holy Spirit would bring my grave oversite to my conscious mind. In the meantime, I looked forward to going to work six days each week and working ten to twelve hours a day. It was very satisfying to be practicing comprehensive dentistry on patients in my own dental office. I was not working for anyone but myself. I never was late and never took off any sick or mental health days. I even encouraged my dental assistant and reception to come to work every day, because I was willing to pay them for all unused sick days at the end of each year.

As the grand opening day for my dental office was approaching, the residents were stopping by the office asking questions and scheduling their dental appointments. So, by the time I begin treating patients, my appointment book was booked up three weeks in advanced. To me this was a very good indication that I had chosen the right location for my dental practice.

I thought my first year had gone very well considering that I was new in the neighborhood. I was meeting all of my business expenses on time. I was a left-handed dentist, and initially my assistant had to get used to assisting me. However, she had adjusted very well and was very good with patients. My receptionist was just the opposite.

Although my receptionist had excellent communication and business skills, she could not spell. I even purchased a dictionary for dummies at her request, but this did not help her. She said she did not know how to find the words in the dictionary since she did not know how to spell the words. I was totally perplexed with her reasoning and was ill-prepared to help her rectify her dilemma. Actually, I was baffled. I had never heard of anyone not being able to look up words in the dictionary and not being able to locate them in my entire life. Maybe I should have requested that she should look for another job, but I didn't. Instead I limited her to non-typing tasks without reducing her salary and advised her to learn how to spell. My office auxiliaries kept me busy, and I enjoyed every minute.

After the first year, I reduced my work schedule to five days each week, because I wanted to spend more time with Robert and the children. Angela had been attending a parochial school since the ninth grade and worked in my office at the front desk. Robert Jr. was busy playing sports on Saturdays. I had time to read books purely for pleasure and relaxation and to socialize with friends more. I was having the best time of my life, or so I thought. My practice was thriving; Robert and I were happily married and the children were busy being normal and healthy children.

Yet, I would be overcome with sadness and negative thoughts would fill my mind for no reason. Over a period of time, these episodes occurred more frequently.

In my free time, I read numerous fictional books of various genres. Reading became my favorite pastime, because I could escape into the stories I was reading. I read every fictional book I could acquire, except horror ones. Because I had been raised to attend church every Sunday, I began to visit different churches with my children every Sunday. I never visited the same ones too frequently so that no one would take notice of me. When the various church clerks would ask all visitors to stand and introduce themselves, I ignored their requests. I had continued this practice many years.

Around the same time, my dental license was up for renewal after two years. The Board of Dental Examiners sent me the renewal application along with a request for proof that I had taken at least 40 credits of continuing educational (CE) courses over the last two years. I had accumulated more than 75 CE credits. I completed the renewal application and mailed it back, accompanied with my renewal fee and proof of all of the CE courses I had taken.

My dental practice was showing steady growth signs during the second and third year (1984 and 1985). Patients who had been placed on three, four, and six months recall were returning for their care. This was a good indication that my dental auxiliaries and I were doing something right, and I was very pleased.

However, in December 1985, I began to feel a void from deep within, as if the void was in my soul, although my relationship with Robert and the children were better than ever. On a Sunday afternoon in autumn, as Robert and I were visiting our friends Betty and John, I shared with Betty that I felt a deep loneliness within my heart and soul. And this loneliness had become a constant presence in my body. One of Betty's and John's male friends overhead our conversation and immediately stated that he felt the same way. For a moment, there was complete silence in the room. After a few minutes had passed, the conversations changed to other topics. And I continued to experience that loneliness.

A couple months later, Daddy, who was living in Alabama, told me that he was in need of some urgent dental care. But I had to promise him that I would make sure he attended Sunday church services and each mid-week prayer services. Of course, I gave Daddy my promise to both of his requests. Immediately, I proceeded to make air flight reservations for Daddy's impending trip. Daddy arrived on January 2, 1986.

On Sunday, January 5th, he and I were on our way to Mount Moriah Baptist Church (MMBC) located on Pleasant Street, Brockton, MA to attend Sunday School and the traditional worship service. However, I made a left turn onto Legion Parkway, parked the car, and proceeded to help Daddy out of the car. I accidently closed both car doors with my car key still in the ignition. I did not tell Daddy I had done this at the time, because I did not want to upset him. However, I said to him that I made a mistake, and we had ended up at the wrong church, which was Messiah Baptist Church (MBC). But I had meant for us to attend MMBC a couple blocks north of us, because I had heard Rev. Neville preach several times in the past when he was the pastor of MBC. Since, Rev. Neville left, MBC has a new pastor and I have never heard him preach. Daddy said since we are here, let's stay. So, we did.

I escorted Daddy into MBC and introduced him to some of the deacons. Then we proceeded to the adult Sunday School class and remained for the traditional worship service. Immediately following the worship service, I escorted Daddy to the fellowship hall for refreshments and fellowshipping with the members. I introduced Daddy to the pastor and mentioned that I would be bringing him on Sundays to Sunday School and worship service.

The pastor immediately asked, "And what about the doctor?" Initially, I had a wide smile on my face, but when the pastor asked me that question, I felt as if my smile had frozen on my face. So, I just continued smiling and said nothing. I was lost for words.

All week long, as Daddy and I traveled to my dental practice, I talked continuously about the sermon I had heard on Sunday while Daddy patiently listened. During our drives back home, I continuously talked about the Sunday sermon. I dreamt about that Sunday sermon.

That sermon consumed my thoughts all of my waking hours and even while I slept. A week later, on Sunday, January 12, 1986, I sensed that God was talking directly to me during the gospel message as it was being preached.

When Pastor Walker said, "The doors of the church are open," I stood and walked up to him and recommitted and rededicated my life to Jesus Christ and offered Pastor Michael Wayne Walker my hand.

However, I was still broken, burdened, and scarred. I was still ashamed, and I still had many questions unanswered. Yet I knew God's love for me had drawn me back. I was in a safe environment, and I was in the right place at the right time. The Word of God says in Proverb 22:6 to train up a child in the way she should go, and when she is old, she will return to it.

I was so thankful to God and very excited about belonging to a community of faith again. When Daddy and I were driving home, I told him that I had recommitted and rededicated my life to God and joined the church. Daddy began smiling and said nothing for a few moments. Then, in a calm voice and while still smiling, he said that he already knew.

I asked Daddy, "How did you already know?" He said he knew God had a hold on me all week because I had talked about the previous sermon every day and several times each day. All I could do was smile. After a few moments, I said thank you, Daddy. I also told Daddy that I was very grateful that he had come to stay with me. I realized that God used my Daddy to bring me back to God.

While Daddy was still living with my family and me, I delved into reading and studying the Bible on a daily basis, meditating on certain scriptures, and attending new members Bible classes. Life for me was absolutely wonderful. Finally, I had returned to the community of faith where I truly belonged, and MBC was the right church for me.

God provided me with a gentle and loving New Member's class teacher, Deacon Jackson, and a very loving and compassionate neighbor, Deacon Harris, who ministered to me as we walked in the mornings. I purposely sought God daily. I arose very early in the morning so that I would have time to pray, read the Bible, and meditate on God's Word. I was baptized in April 1986.

Most of the time, I felt fine. Yet some days, I thought of negative things that made me sad. One day I was busy treating a patient, and all of a sudden, my mind wandered onto something very unpleasant that disturbed me. As soon as I had an opportunity, I called Pastor

Walker, and he advised me to concentrate on reading First and Second Corinthians, Ephesians, and Philippians. He said those were viewed as happy books and that I needed to empty all of the useless information from my mind and replace it with the Word of God. I instantly remembered reading numerous books for the last 15 years just to occupy my mind, so that I did not have time to think about the past.

I knew I had much work before me as I remembered all of those fictional books I had read over the last 15 years. I exhibited amazing zeal and fervor for God's Word and love for God that only other believers in Jesus Christ understood. I eagerly took and completed every Bible class offered at Messiah. I attended and completed every seminar and workshop held at Messiah. Whenever my schedule permitted, I attended and completed other workshops held at other Baptist churches. I had this exciting thirst to learn and know God better. The only way I knew to accomplish this was through reading and studying the Bible, meditating on God's Word, attending Bible Study and classes with other believers, attending and participating in worship services, and fellowshipping with other believers.

As the months passed, I called the church secretary and scheduled meetings with Pastor Walker. From the onset, I informed Pastor Walker that I was not going to tip toe through the tulips and attempt to clean up anything but rather I would tell him exactly what was on my mind. And I did just that. I asked Pastor Walker tough questions, and to many, he would say he did not know. I respected Pastor Walker for being honest. Yet, I continued to ask him tough questions. During one of our earlier meetings, I told Pastor Walker about me being raped, which resulted in me giving birth to Angela. I shared the details of how I felt after the rape and how I prayed to God every night to allow me to sleep into eternity. But every morning, God awakened me. I told Pastor Walker that I had asked God numerous questions regarding this heinous experience and the numerous other challenges I've had to endure. Pastor Walker always gave me several scriptures to read, to study, and to meditate on. These meetings were a tremendous help to me through the years.

Through God's grace, mercy, and love, I received some of the answers to many of my questions, although some of them remained unanswered. Yet whenever new questions arose, I told God and asked God for answers. Whenever I had doubt, I asked God to be my strength and remove all of my doubts, because only God could, since there was nothing too hard for God. I chose to believe and trust God in every aspect of my life, including my money, time, talents, and expertise.

With assistance, prayers, and the support of my family and members of the community of faith, I became victorious, whole, and healthy in Jesus Christ. Their embracing attitudes and loving spirits lead me to unload everything onto God. God's mercy, grace, and love healed my body and mind. God gave me a spirit of compassion for others. I believe many individuals suffer due to no fault of their own, just as I had suffered. Jesus took up our infirmities and carried our sorrows, yet we considered him "stricken by God and afflicted."

I fervently prayed to God to direct me in the ways that were pleasing to God and to fill my dreams with God's presence. God heard and answered my prayers. I made sure I had pen and paper on hand to write notes during every sermon. I took up the habit of journaling as suggested by Pastor Walker, which enabled me to see how God was working in my life even more than was evident to me prior to my journaling. I began to reflect a full and active life in Jesus Christ. My faith was not only about me, but it was about the community of faith and of all of God's children, whether they knew it or not. I had begun to write down prayers prayed for specific individuals and for God's children both far and near as I witnessed God's answered prayers through my journaling.

After Daddy's dental treatment was completed and he was pleased with the outcome, he informed me that it was time for him to return to Alabama. I was enjoying having Daddy living with Robert, the children, and me, so I did not receive this news well at all. I was very distressed, and so I consulted Pastor Walker. He advised me to consent to my Daddy's request without further hesitation. I cried, but I consented and made Daddy's flight reservations to Alabama. After Daddy left, the cooking and food shopping again became dreaded chores, and I struggled doing them.

Cooking for Daddy was much easier for me, because I had cooked for him the same way as I cooked foods for myself: the healthy way and not for taste. Daddy was always appreciative and never complained. On the other hand, Robert and the children had constantly complained about certain entrees that I had cooked and those they disliked. I readily admitted that I was not a good cook and never cared to become one. However, I proceeded to learn to cook foods that my children would eat, such as Kraft's macaroni and cheese, cheese burgers, hot dogs, broccoli, string beans, corn on the cob, to name a few. Going forward, the complaints from my family about the meals ceased, because I had learned to cook selected entrees and side dishes reasonably well.

Overall, I was pleased with Robert and our relationship. Angela had graduated from Cardinal Spellman High School and was attending Mount Holyoke College in South Hadley, MA. Robert Jr., on the other hand, was being a typical active boy and busy playing year round sports in the Pop Warner league in Easton, and preparing to take the independent exam for acceptance into a private school. But my dental office was a different story.

The first three years of practicing general dentistry were good years for a new practice. But by the beginning of the fourth year, which was in late 1986, everything went downhill. There was a drastic increase in patients' no shows, a drastic increase in patients unprepared to pay on the days services were rendered, a drastic increase in patients saying they forgot their checkbooks, and there was a drastic increase in bounced checks. At this pace, I knew it would not be long before I had to lay off my dental personnel and close my office permanently. The inevitable finally happened. I had no other choice but to close my dental practice in less than five years after its grand opening.

As the result of me closing my dental office on February 28, 1987, I was left with a large debt, which I was unable to repay. The bank had threatened to take me to court for non-payment. At this juncture, all eight credit cards were maxed out in my attempts to keep my dental practice operating and hoping things would turn around for the best. I was unable to pay the monthly payments due on those several credit cards. Now nine banks were calling me constantly about those overdue payments. I promised all nine banks that I would repay all of my outstanding debts as soon as I began to make some money.

In less than six months, my credit ratings had fallen to an all-time low. I stopped bothering to check my credit score. When the eight credit card banks called me asking about payments, I told them all the same thing: that I promised to pay, in full, all the money I owed. But, it was going to take me some time to begin earning money. Finally, I told all nine banks to take me to court, because I did not care anymore. In addition, I told them that as long as none of them had authority over my life, then they may continue threatening me for non-payment as much as they like. But, one day after I had paid all of them back, they would be begging me to apply for their credit cards. In total, I was over $100,000 in debt and had no prospect of a job.

As I was contemplating my next steps, I realized that I had neglected to tell God all about my dental practice plans back in 1982-83. I remembered that I never asked the Holy Spirit for guidance in any of those challenging decisions and that I had made them all by myself. I regretted what I had done and asked for God's forgiveness. I felt much better afterwards.

Closing my dental practice had been very painful. Mentally, I was not ready to seek a dental associate position in another dental practice. I needed time to recover from this grave disappointment, and so I became gainfully employed at Equifax Credit Bureau for approximately four months. This job took my mind off dentistry the majority of the time during the day, and in the evenings, I taught a "Two Year Discipleship" classes, "Through the Bible in One Year" Bible classes, and I sang in the adult choir.

After four months, I quit my Equifax job and began interviewing for a dental associate job in private dental practices. I had no difficulty being hired as a dental associate. The problems were that all of them were very disappointing and unsuccessful, except one. The worst one was in Hanover, Massachusetts located in a shopping mall. After working full days each week, my take home salary was $184/week. The second worst one was at the Westgate Mall in Brockton, Massachusetts. At that one, I walked out and never looked back after about an hour on my first day, because the owner expected me to treatment non-English-speaking dental patients without an interpreter. I am monolingual.

The most productive and rewarding of them all was the dental office in New Bedford, Massachusetts, which was owned by Dr. Cabral. For the very first time, I had opportunities to earn salaries I felt I deserved as a practicing dental medical doctor. The dental office was located on a main street in New Bedford, Massachusetts, and the majority of my dental patients spoke Portuguese as their first language. The receptionist spoke English, Spanish, and Portuguese, one dental assistant spoke English and Portuguese, and the other dental assistant spoke only English. I felt right at home, although I spoke only English. Yet I knew the universal language very well, and I used it to my advantage: smile. Mama and Daddy had taught that a smile would always help me accomplish much more than a frown. Mama and Daddy were correct.

The office personnel managed the office exceedingly well, and I could not have had more efficient dental assistants.

One day in 1988, I was alone with God and my thoughts as I drove to New Bedford to my job. I heard God's audible voice, which was soft and clear in my right ear. I quickly looked in the rear view mirror, checking the back seat. On that day, God called me to the ministry of preaching and teaching the good news of Jesus Christ. But I doubted the call.

I told Robert that God had called me to preach the gospel of Jesus Christ a few weeks later. He said he did not want me to become a preacher. I did not know how to discern his response. So, I said nothing. A couple months later, his sister Elnora was in Boston for a conference. Robert and I drove in one evening to see her. When Elnora and I were alone, I told her that God had called me to preach. She was silent on the matter. I did not know how to discern her silence. So, I said nothing. I wondered to myself that both Robert and Elnora thought I was unworthy of such a noble call, and I did not measure up to what a minister of the gospel of Jesus Christ looked and behaved like.

Henceforth, I did not acknowledge God's call inwardly or outwardly. However, I did accept several speaking engagements as a guest speaker at different churches. Sometimes, I was thankful to God for calling me, and I felt confident about what I needed to do. Other times, I did not feel thankful and lacked confidence.

During this time, I was still working as a dental associate in Dr. Cabral's office. I was very content as I provided quality comprehensive dental care to my dental patients. Although these patients worked in low to medium paying jobs, they honored their payment obligations each time they received their paychecks. Another reason I was content with my job was that the patients willingly accepted the best treatment options I offered. They did not want alternative treatment plans. Therefore, they chose payment plans in order to receive the best dental care. You see, I practiced dentistry from the philosophy of prevention, restoring dental health, function, and esthetics. And this was the first time in my life as a licensed general dentist that all of the patients accepted the best treatment options, and I was utilizing all of skills TUSDM had taught me.

The patient population in New Bedford was a perfect fit for me, and I thoroughly looked forward to each day working there. Unfortunately, due to scheduling conflicts, I could no longer cover Dr. Cabral's work schedule as I had previously done when he vacationed in Cape Verdes each year, and therefore, I had to leave and seek a dental associate position elsewhere. By this time, I was not too concerned about finding another position, because I was an experienced dentist with complete confidence in my managerial abilities and clinical skills.

In the meantime, in July 1989, Robert and I went on our first cruise. We flew to Miami and were taken to the Port of Miami by bus. It was extremely hot and humid in Miami. While on the cruise, we visited the Bahamas, Saint Martin, Saint John, and Saint Thomas. Robert and I had never in our lives seen so much delicious-looking foods. I made sure I went to the fitness center daily, so that I would not gain any weight, but it was a challenge. There were different shows and performances each night, and there were movies shown at various times during the day and night. The cruise ship had to wait until it was a specific distance from the Port of Miami before it opened its casino. This was the first time I had ever been in a casino, and I was excited about being in one. We decided that we would take a cruise at least every two years, and we did.

Robert and I had dinner reservations for second seating. After the first night, we dressed up for dinner, and during the Captain's Night, we readily took a photo with him. I would say that we did everything first time cruisers did. Many of the members from my church were on the cruise along with Pastor Walker, his wife Paulette, and their two children. Pastor Walker's mom and aunt were on the cruise, too. In addition, there were several people from Dallas, Texas who also knew the Walkers. Pastor Walker and Paulette were originally from Dallas, Texas.

Once we were back in Massachusetts, I kept myself very busy and avoided making a decision about doing something about God's call to me to preach. Whenever I mustered up the nerve to schedule an appointment with Pastor Walker, I would cancel each time. Although God had healed my brokenness and pain, I felt that I was unworthy of preaching the gospel of Jesus Christ. At that time, I owed over $56,000 from my unsuccessful dental practice, and I owed $33,000 to eight credit card accounts. I thought to myself, who would listen to me? My professional life was in shambles, and I had far too many unpaid credit card accounts.

After leaving Dr. Cabral's dental office, I ended up at the worst dental office of them all, which was in Hanover, Massachusetts. I had plenty of free time each day.

So, I would go to Dunkin for black coffee and read the Boston Globe from cover to cover. On one occasion, I saw a help wanted ad that said dentist wanted at a community health center in Providence, Rhode Island.

Immediately, I called that health center and scheduled an interview with the medical director for the following day. The interview went very well, and I was hired on the spot, although there was a little matter that I had to address. When I had passed the Northeast Regional Board (NERB) in 1981, it covered 22 states. However, I had only maintained an active dental license in Massachusetts. I needed to activate my RI license before I could begin the new position as the dental coordinator at Capitol Hill Community Health Center (CHHC), Providence, Rhode Island. So, I arranged to take the written Rhode Island dental exam and paid the fee. In 1990, I began providing comprehensive dental care to the patients in Providence, RI within two weeks after first reading the help wanted ad.

Again, I had an adequate and steady monthly income. As to be expected, the dental needs of the community were greater than one dentist could handle. My daily work schedule was so highly overbooked that my dental assistants and I never ended on time. Three days each week, we were scheduled to work from 8:30 AM until 5:00 PM, and two days each week we were scheduled to work from 11:00 AM until 9:00 PM. On many days, we left the health center around 6:30 PM and 10:30 PM or later. On several occasions, Robert would call the health center inquiring about my whereabouts. As always, I was too busy to talk directly to him. So, I always instructed one of my assistants to inform my husband that I would call him back as soon as I finished treating the last patient. Fortunately, my drive home late at night usually was only 30 minutes.

Although the workload at CHHC was very demanding, I enjoyed being very busy each day. Again, I was providing quality dental care to patients in an underserviced and underrepresented community. I had reached my professional goal in this aspect, and I did not have the responsibilities of paying the dental practice overhead expenses; the federal government funded this community health center. However, there were some professional disadvantages by working in a community health center. First, there were several procedures the patients could not afford, which I was thoroughly qualified to provide. Second, my daily work schedule was always double and triple booked because of the unreliability of some patients. Third, on days when all scheduled patients kept their appointments, my dental assistants and I were overwhelmed. Fourth, patients' requests to be added to the wait list became so extensive that I abolished the wait list all together. I instructed all dental personnel to say Dr. Howard was only accepting children as new patients. Honestly, I could not say no to any child in need of dental care.

Since I was overwhelmed at work, I needed something that I could concentrate on. Since reading and attending school have been enjoyable for me, I enrolled in Andover-Newton Theological Seminary's (ANTS) evening classes in 1992. My first paper in theology was due three weeks after my enrollment. I completed my paper and submitted it on time. The next week, I was ten minutes late arriving to my theology class, and I was dumbfounded to discover that my theology professor was criticizing my paper to the class as I took my seat. I did not know what to do, although I forced myself not to cry. After this class was over, I went to the Admissions Office and withdrew. It was exactly one month after my enrollment.

After working at CHHC for three years, which was in 1993, I accidentally banged the backside of my right hand against a dental cabinet. My hand hurt profusely, but I was so heavily booked that I barely had time to knowledge the pain and continued to treat patients. By the end of the day, my right hand was hurting so badly that I was very concerned about it. I pondered several what 'if thoughts' all at once. Too many years have passed for me to recall the exact order of my thoughts. But, I thought what if I had permanently injured my hand and I could not practice dentistry anymore? I thought about the consequences of losing my job. I thought about being unable to pay off my debt from my unsuccessful dental practice and credit cards. I was overwhelmed with many what ifs. So, I chose to say nothing to anyone, except my dental assistants, and continued to work every day for the next two weeks. However, I did tell my husband immediately after arriving home the same day I banged my hand.

By the end of two weeks, Robert literally had to help me bathe and get out of the shower. I could no longer withstand the pain. So, I scheduled an appointment with one of the PCP's at CHHC. I was losing strength in my right arm and in constant pain. I was referred to a specialist, and the specialist referred me to a physical therapist. I was placed on workers compensation, because I was unable to practice dentistry anymore. The weekly workers compensation allotment was so small that I could barely pay for the COBRA insurance and my outstanding debts. Financially, times were very tough. Over the next three years, I underwent two surgeries and physical therapy sessions twice per week.

Since I was unable to work, I was available to teach Bible classes on weekdays and evenings. I took advantage of being available to teach. Pastor Walker was very pleased that I was utilizing my time teaching Bible classes. I found myself in demand, and I enjoying teaching. As it turned out, the Holy Spirit had given me multiple spiritual gifts. At the time, my working spiritual gifts were teaching, administration, and mercy. My waiting spiritual gifts were preaching and generosity.

Pastor Walker encouraged all believers to be involved in the community. I heard the call, stepped up to the plate, and got involved in the community-at-large. A group of church members and Pastor Walker gathered together and formed the Jubilee Political Action Committee (JPAC) in early 1992. I stepped up to the opportunity and became the Executive Director of JPAC. In addition, MBC had joined the Brockton Interfaith Community (BIC) when it was first established in 1991. Initially, I was not involved with BIC, except to attend all of their action meetings, which occurred at least two or three times each year. Due to the demands of my job at

CHHC, I was unavailable to attend the regular scheduled meetings whether they were biweekly or monthly.

With me being unable to work, I delved into community service with zeal and fortitude determined to make a difference in God's world. I believed that it was my responsibility to participate in the public arena to help transform God's world into what it should be. JPAC held its monthly meetings on Sundays at 6:00 PM. We had good attendance and participation at these meetings. It was decided that for us to be most effective in our efforts, we should decide on two social justice initiatives. JPAC's initiatives were: 1) To increase the number of police officers of color in the City of Brockton, and 2) To increase the number of teachers of color in the Brockton Public Schools.

Within one year after JPAC's inception, JPAC had been instrumental in getting 14 persons of color hired. Thirteen were teachers of color and one was an 82-year-old female senior who was hired to work in the nursery at the high school. Those teenage parents needed everything she had to offer to help them with their parenting skills. After every meeting with the school superintendent, I would update Pastor Walker on what had occurred. I even confessed to him that I had exaggerated the actual number of active working members of JPAC. My rationale was to never give information to the opponent(s) that would undermine our effectiveness. This strategy worked successfully while I was the Executive Director of JPAC.

Since MBC was a member of BIC, JPAC served in dual roles in addressing social justice initiatives in the City of Brockton, and we became two united groups working on multiple social justice initiatives. This resulted in increased attention and effectiveness in our citywide action meetings, because these large numbers of attendees represented registered voters. And politicians knew they needed registered voters' support.

After a little more than three years of treatment to my right hand, the specialist informed me that I had regained 80 percent of function, but the 20 percent I had lost made my right arm too weak to stabilize patients' heads during their dental treatment. In addition, two of my fingers on my right hand had continuous paresthesia. So, I made the decision that I would seek a teaching position since there was nothing wrong with my brain. I had taught students before at Forsyth, and besides, one of my working spiritual gifts was teaching.

6

A New Beginning

Robert Jr. had graduated from high school and was attending Colgate University in Hamilton, New York. This meant that Robert and I were empty nesters, and it felt great!

In the meantime, I called TUSDM and scheduled an appointment with the Dean. Prior to my appointment, I had taken my resume to a friend who owned a printing company to be updated. My appointment went exceedingly well, and I was hired as a full-time clinical instructor in the Department of General Dentistry.

During the first year, I was also able to work part-time at a facility operated by the Department of Youth Services (DYS) providing dental care to male youths living there. Now, I had two steady incomes coming in. I put the extra money toward my outstanding debts and became debt-free by the end of 1996. It had taken me nine years to pay off eight credit card's debt and my former dental office debt. Henceforth, I was determined to charge what I could afford to pay off on a monthly basis.

The DYS was located in the YMC in Brockton. All of these children had been removed from their homes for various reasons. Some of them would not attend school on a regular basis and others were constantly in trouble with the police. The youngest child in this facility was 12-years-old. When I looked into his eye, my heart ached for him and his situation he had gotten himself in. He was just a baby. This 12-year-old said that he had gotten tired of being bullied every day in school. So, he decided to bring a gun to school just to threaten the boy who was constantly bullying him. Someone reported him to the principal of his school, and he was removed from his parents' home and placed in the care of DYS. My brain could not comprehend this young child's reasoning. I thought to myself: how could a 12-year-old go and purchase an illegal gun?

Because my life was proceeding so well, I enrolled in Gordon-Conwell Theological Seminary's (GCST) evening classes in September of 1996. I was determined to complete seminary school this time. Well, after one week into the program, I withdrew because of the following reason. During one of my classes, my professor asked each seminary student to name our favorite animal and why. Well, I am a lover of people and not animals. As a matter of fact, I have never had a pet animal of any kind. When it was my turn to share, I said that I actually didn't have a favorite animal, but if I must choose one, it would be a deer because they run away whenever people approach them, and they stand very majestically as they roam in the wild. My professor called me an animal hater that night in class. I have never purposely injured any animal in my entire lifetime, and to be called an animal hater by an ordained clergyman was perplexing and unacceptable.

I labeled my first year teaching at TUSDM as my honeymoon year. It was an absolute pleasure working there. Morale was very high among the faculty members. Several of my older colleagues took me under their wings and guided me through the entire process of being a success at TUSDM. I regarded them as my mentors. I was very grateful, and I eagerly expressed my gratitude to each of them. I had never in my entire life had as many individuals all at one time willing to help me.

There was no envy or jealousy among them, although one of them by the name of Arthur asked, "Margaret, how did you get your teaching job?"

I responded, "The same as you did, Arthur." Every mentor tirelessly answered all of my questions and gave hands-on demonstrations whenever they were necessary. Believe me, I asked them numerous questions and patiently waited for their answers.

During my first teaching year, my nickname became Sunshine, because I was always smiling, greeting everyone with kind words, and exhibiting a positive attitude. Some of my colleagues said that when I walked in a room, it became brighter, and everyone desired to behave better in my presence. I was very grateful to God that God was using me to bring out the good in others. My life was finally beautiful in all areas. I was at peace because of God's love and healing power.

As the years passed, I had come to realize that there seemed to always be a period of calm before a storm. A turbulent storm was on the horizon and was fast approaching TUSDM, and the entire clinical faculty members were unaware of this fast approaching turbulent storm. As far as we were concerned, all was well at TUSDM, although there had been a comprehensive revision of the dental program during my first year of teaching. Since I was teaching in the clinic primarily, the changes in the curricula did not affect my job. The dental clinical changes implemented were for the best for all stakeholders: students, patients, faculty, and school. Actually, I had no complaints and enjoyed working at TUSDM.

I decided to enroll in a Master of Education degree program in January 1997 at Cambridge College located in Cambridge. The worst thing that happened was my sister, Arola, died unexpectedly that January. Family members from far and near, along with members from my home church, attended her home going celebration and funeral. This time all of the Williams' siblings knew how to make funeral arrangements. My life was being touched by death in ways that I could never prepare for. Arola was only 58-years-old when she died. My large family was beginning to shrink. I began to think that there was so much work left for me to do, and my time remaining alive was becoming shorter and shorter. I became restless in my spirit. So, I kept busy with my family and few close friends. I scheduled more frequent trips to Alabama and Mississippi to visit Robert and my families. Robert and I made it a priority to spend more time with our families.

At the end of my first year, TUSDM promoted me to assistant professor. The Executive Dean implemented a group practice model for the dental clinic and chose ten different group practices. I was appointed as practice coordinator over group six named the yellow group. Remember, I was called Sunshine by many of my colleagues.

Also in 1997, one of my colleagues, Aida, asked me to help her mentor the dental assistants who were completing their dental assistant externship at TUSDM. I enthusiastically agreed. Aida was a periodontist who had had begun teaching at TUSDM a couple of years before me. I even began going to their high school, Madison Park, and gave presentations several times each year. I had known the director of the dental assistance program for several years, because we had been classmates at Forsyth. Her name was Ruby.

Each entering dental class was assigned to specific group practices. In this way, all dental students had opportunities to get to know their practice coordinators well in advance of scheduling and treating patients in the clinic. All assigned students had two years to interact with their practice coordinators as often as possible without being concerned about not knowing what they should know but don't. I was appointed to the Infection

Control and Admissions Committees. Someone recommended me without my knowledge, and I discovered this through TUSDM's email. I knew to just show up at the scheduled time and that is just what I did.

Doing orientation week for the incoming class, all of the practice coordinators were scheduled to greet and meet their assigned dental students. I took advantage of these opportunities. With my positive demeanor, friendly and genuine, wide smile, and beautiful white teeth, the majority of dental students felt at ease with me immediately. This approach worked each year, and all I did was to continue to improve it as I used it. Actually, I was a natural with students, patients, my colleagues, and staff. I am not being arrogant. It was just that I was very comfortable in my own skin when it came to interacting with everyone. I established such an outstanding reputation that even one of TUSDM Board of Trustees told me that he wanted his daughter to be assigned to my group practice. I was very pleased with his comment.

As a matter of fact, my group practice was used as a model by the TUSDM's Admissions when discussing the group practice model during the applicants' interviews. The Dean of Admissions asked me on several occasions to meet with the entire first year class during orientation. I accepted his invitations until they interfered with my other assigned responsibilities. I did not want to jeopardize my job.

I was enjoying the classes at Cambridge College, because I was confirming to myself that I was an excellent teacher. I just did not know the names of the systems and theories to apply to my teaching styles, but my professors at Cambridge College did. For the first time since attending school in Alabama, I felt that I was actually being taught and not been given the responsibility of teaching myself. My college advisor, one of my many professors, was a bar certified attorney but had chose to teach rather than practice law. I counted myself very fortunate and blessed to have her in both roles.

After the first year, it was as if a wicked witch from the west had come to TUSDM. Actually, I made efforts to be a team player, but the non-team players had louder voices and more complaints and low morale among the faculty became the norm. The turbulent storm had finally arrived at TUSDM, and it appeared to be there to stay.

I continued to establish myself in a very positive light in regards to teaching and mentoring, and I was known to be trustworthy, truthful, and accepting of everyone.

Yet, I did not receive positive written evaluations from my assigned dental students, although my group of students received the most awards during TUSDM's senior dinners, had the highest on time graduation, and the highest percentage for passing their dental licensing exam, such as the Northeast Regional Board (NERB) given by the Board of Dental Examiners. It baffled me that my students would not write positive comments when they completed their evaluations at the end of the year. In January 1998, I completed the Master of Education Program at Cambridge College. To celebrate my graduation, Robert and I went on a cruise to Alaska during my August vacation, and in April 1999, we traveled to England, France, and Italy. Overall, my life was very good. In January 2000, I enrolled in a Public Health degree program at Tufts University School of Medicine (TUSM).

To my surprise, there was no written manual for practice coordinators to teach their students on how to become good to excellent diagnosticians. It was essential for all students to master this diagnosis and treatment planning skills before picking up any dental instruments to administer dental treatment.

So, I began to formulate and write educational models in my area of expertise, which was Oral Diagnosis and

Treatment Planning, and I improved on these models each year. I consistently taught my students using these educational models. I gave them hard copies of each model with explanations of each step. During our scheduled monthly meetings, these models became known as rubrics and were discussed in detail. And all students' concerns were addressed.

During my 2001 summer vacation, Robert and I traveled to Italy. We visited Venice, Florence, and Rome. When 9/11 occurred, Robert and I had only been back in the United States two weeks. Gloom filled the air, and a nervous tension and fear gripped everyone on that fateful afternoon. The patients, students, staff, and faculty members were visibly upset. At the time, I was in the laboratory assisting one of my students, and when I returned to the clinic, I was stunned to learn about the terrorists' attacks on the twin towers of the World Trade Center in New York and the Pentagon just outside of Washington, DC.

Many of my colleagues felt that their sense of security and safety had been destroyed forever after 9/11. I, on the other hand, did not feel the same way as they did and never would. I explained to many of them that I and countless others like me never relied on people to keep us safe and secure but rather we depend on God, our Keeper, our Deliverer, and our Way Maker, because countless people living in the world are not color blind.

So, I said to them, "Welcome to my world." It became the norm at TUSDM to hear people say God bless America. To date, I still say God bless all people, because I know God favors us all, and it is people who discriminate, who establish invisible walls, and who justify systems that cause divisions and injustices among God's people.

After 9/11, I implemented an open door policy so that I was more accessible to help my students through this unsettling period and to eliminate their excuses. I would arrive to work an hour early each morning on my workdays and usually left an hour late. I was the only practice coordinator who bent over backward to do everything in my power to help dental students become the best dentists they humanly could be. Yet, when it came time for my students to evaluate me at the end of each year, many of them wrote very mean spirited and negative comments. It happened so often that the Chair of my department said to me that there was nothing I could do about it, because some students just did not like me. I continued teaching each student to first, do no harm, and second, to provide the best dental care to each patient as if they were treating themselves. Their attitudes remained a mystery to me. Outwardly, I never discussed the negative evaluations with anyone at work since the Chair of my department had said there was nothing I could do about it. Inwardly, I remained perplexed.

By this time, there was some discord among the dental faculty regarding salary disparities. TUSDM's faculty salaries were one of the lowest when compared to other dental school. TUSDM hired a registered nurse to update and implement the quality control protocol in the dental clinic. The registered nurse's salary was more than $20,000 than our salaries, mine included. The 20 practice coordinators signed a letter addressed to the Dean expressing our dissatisfaction about our low salaries and requested a meeting.

During that meeting, we made it clear that TUSDM could do without the recently hired registered nurse, but TUSDM could not exist without licensed dentists in good standing with the Board of Dental Examiners, because all dental students were learning dentistry under our licenses when they provided dental care to patients. Besides, a licensed dentist could have been hired to update and implement the quality control protocol for the clinic.

The Dean agreed and advised the Chair of the General Dentistry and Dean of Clinics to schedule individual appointments with us. As a group, all of the practice coordinators agreed to stand together through to the end just as we were united when all of us signed the letter addressed to the Dean. Well, some of us remained united, but there were some who negotiated their own private deals. I honored our original agreement, but some of the other faculty did not. After this betrayal, I refused to participate in any future group negotiations. I was very disappointed with the outcome, because my annual salary remained too low.

I was selected to participate on one of TUSDM's accreditation committees within a couple of years after being hired. I do not recall the exact year. However, I was assigned to one of the strategic committees. The official accreditation committee was scheduled to come to evaluate TUSDM in the month of March in less than two years. During the official accreditation process, I was asked several questions about the availability of faculty development at TUSDM. I truthfully said that TUSDM provided opportunities regularly each year for faculty development. I attended the National Dental Association annual dental conference each year and all of my expenses incurred were paid by TUSDM. Afterwards, the Chair of General Dentistry, Dr. Mehta, informed me that my responses about faculty development had impressed the accreditation committee immensely and resulted in TUSDM receiving high marks.

Three years later, Aida asked me to co-author a professional paper for publication. I agreed. I became Institutional Review Board (IRB) certified before venturing into this co-writing of a professional research paper. Afterward, the paper was accepted and published. To date, this is the only paper that has my name on it and has been published. I admit that this research paper was not well written. There was nothing wrong with the research aspect of the paper. It was just that Aida's first language was Spanish, and she refused to allow any editing of the final version of our paper or follow through on my recommendation to allow an objective person to proof read our paper before submitting it for publication. I knew that, although English was my first language, I still needed a qualified individual to edit and proofread our paper before submitting it for final publication. To this day, I do not understand why the New

England Journal of General Dentistry did not thoroughly peruse our paper and recommend corrections of some sort before proceeding to its publication. Oh, well, that was water under the bridge.

In 2002, I received a Master's degree in Public Health with a concentration in public health policies and programs. I was in my sixth year of teaching at TUSDM. At the end of the fiscal school year, I was promoted to the position of an Associate Professor in the General Dentistry Department but without any additional increase in salary. As a matter of fact, I did not receive any additional salary increases while teaching at TUSDM for either of my master's degree. Yet, I realized that by me having two advanced degrees, it made me more marketable overall. I reasoned that maybe one day I would choose to seek employment elsewhere. One never knows for sure.

By end of the school year in 2002, I had gotten used to unfavorable evaluations from my students. Yet, face to face, they smiled and spoke favorable words to me. I decided that it was their problems and not mine, and I refused to internalize anyone else's problems. I had enough in my own backpack to handle.

Each year after 2002, all of the other years were replicas of each other. Some faculty members left TUSDM, and new faculty members were hired. Some faculty members were even fired. I never concerned myself with the possibility of being fired. First, I knew I was doing my job exceedingly well, and second, I was the only African American full-time Assistant Professor employed at TUSDM.

I was not aware of any of the other faculty in my department who were interested in receiving any advance degrees. Out of the 24 practice coordinators, only four of us had an additional degree(s), and I was the only one with two master's degrees. To my knowledge, the remaining 20 practice coordinators were perfectly content with only their D.M.D degrees.

Again, I enrolled in Andover-Newton Theological Seminary (ANTS) in September 2007. I was excited about being able to put my previous painful and negative experience behind me. Before starting my classes at ANTS this time, I went and shared my previous experience with one of the theologians at ANTS. She assured me that other students had similar experiences with the same professor and informed me that that professor no longer taught at ANTS. I was taking three classes and doing very well in all of them. But Daddy died in October, which was only a month after I had begun.

When Mama had died, Daddy was the rock for me. Now, there was no one I could depend on as I had depended on Daddy. All of the Williams' siblings were numbed and got through Daddy's home going celebration and funeral the best we could under the circumstances. We had fallen apart emotionally and suffered in silence for months. Thankfully, Robert understood what I was going through since both of his parents had been dead for several years. Someone from ANTS called me after two weeks to find out if I would be returning to the program. I told them that currently I felt that I did not have the mental and physical stamina to continue the program, I withdrew from ANTS for the second time.

It was 2008 when I applied for the position of Division Head in the Department of General Dentistry. Of the 24 practice coordinators, I had the most advanced degrees, the highest on time graduation, and highest number of students receiving awards each year. I was confident that I would be hired as the next Division Head. Unfortunately, I did not get the job. I was very disappointed.

However, my life continued, and I concentrated on my job while at work and on my family and myself during my personal time. I never answered any emails from my students during my personal time. I totally disconnected from all work-related issues during my personal time.

Robert and I were doing a lot of traveling and taking advantage of every opportunity availed to us. We were either going on cruises or visiting the different states in the United States. After 9/11, Robert didn't want to travel abroad visiting any foreign countries. Therefore, we spent many vacations in the different Caribbean Islands, Bermuda, Alaska, and the United States.

In 2008, Cassie arranged to gather all of the Williams' siblings together. It was heavy on her heart that we did not spend time together regularly, except for annual family reunions. Our extended families were huge. So, one can imagine the time limitation all of the Williams' siblings had to gather together during those family reunions. Therefore, it became a regular occasion for all of us to meet in Dothan, Alabama at least three to four times each year. Personally, I was thrilled, although I was the only one who had traveled the farthest and spent more money each time. Yet, it was worth it, and I considered all of our gatherings pure joy.

Through the years, I continued to be very busy in my home church ministries in various capacities and involved in social justice initiates in the community.

Early in 2012, I told Robert that God still had a call to the ministry on my life. He looked directly at me and said that he was okay with that. I just stared back at him for a few seconds. Then, I asked him if he was all right with me preaching, why didn't he come and tell me when he was all right with it? Robert asked me what I meant by that. I said when I told him in 1988 that God had called to preach, he said adamantly that he did not want me to preach. Then, when we drove into Boston to visit Elnora a short time afterward, I told her the same thing and she remained silent. I was perplexed. I wondered if the both of them had a discussion and felt that I did not measure up to what a preacher should be. Robert told me that I should not have paid attention to him back in 1988. I asked if he was kidding me. And did he realize what I had been through these last 24 years? Robert remained silent, and I felt like screaming and throwing a temper tantrum. But I did neither. I just stood silently, looking directly back at Robert as I shook my head in silence.

I scheduled and canceled several appointments with Pastor Walker over the next couple of months. Finally, I scheduled another appointment in August 2012 and kept it. During our meeting, I told Pastor Walker that God had called me to preach and teach the gospel of

Jesus Christ, and I had known this for a long time. Pastor Walker just sat there and listened.

When I finished talking, Pastor Walker smiled and agreed with me. I was relieved and elated. I believe Pastor Walker already knew I had been called to the ministry, and he had been patiently waiting for me to tell him.

Pastor Walker assigned me a mentor by the name of Deacon Linda Ross. A few months later, Pastor Walker appointed me to be the Resource Minister of MBC. One of my responsibilities was to be the liaison for the church and the community. I remained in this position for one year.

7

I Remain a Work in Progress

I entered the American Baptist Churches of MA School of Ministry (TABCOMSoM) located in Groton, Massachusetts soon after I had consulted with Pastor Walker about God's call on my life. This three-year program was just what I needed, because the classes were small, and the other students attending SoM were very easy to get to know. Each school year was from February until November. The SoM had a circular curriculum, which meant that seminarians could enter the program for the first time during any semester. I entered the SoM in February 2013. The first semester included Old Testament, theology, and preaching technics. My SoM professors scheduled guest ordained ministers to give seminars on different subjects regularly on Saturday afternoons. I had no problems with the any of my classes. Seminarians ate all meals together on weekends. After our dinners on Fridays, time was scheduled for sharing and fellowshipping with each other.

During my attendance at the first sharing and fellowshipping session, all of us were asked to introduce ourselves and give a brief bio. We were instructed that we could share whatever we felt comfortable sharing. I felt very comfortable and at ease as each student shared. After about an hour into our session, I raised my hand and Rev. Bardon acknowledged my raised hand. I was led by the Holy Spirit to share my rape experiences with everyone gathered at that first session, although it was the first meeting. I felt no shame or embarrassment as I shared this cruel and heinous act with the students and professors. I was very grateful for the environment of our sharing and fellowshipping session. After all those years and for the first time, I was able to share that heinous experience without shame or disgust with persons I did not know. I felt no hate for the perpetrator anymore. I was free at last. Thank God! I had received complete healing from the heinous rape, which had occurred more than 46 years previously during that Friday evening session. And all of us in attendance developed a special bonding for each other.

As I continued in TABCOM SoM, I discovered that this program was harder than it first appeared. I had only two weeks to prepare a five-minute sermon. At first, I thought that preparing a five-minute sermon was a piece of cake. I was sadly mistaken. Besides, I am not good at baking cakes. This should have told me something. As it turned out, the first sermon I preached was absolutely awful. After I gave my first sermon, the students and professors shared their opinions. I was not defensive in the least because I knew the only direction for me was to improve. Henceforth, my preaching techniques and presentations improved drastically after each future sermon.

During the last month of my first semester, I was given a summer fieldwork assignment. I had to preach at least four sermons over the summer. Well, I did not know four different pastors of churches, although I knew numerous associate ministers just like me. I needed to obtain permission to preach from pastors of churches. I knew Pastor Walker would grant me one opportunity to preach, which he did.

So, I searched the Internet for all First Baptist Churches within a 20-mile radius from my home. After searching the Internet, I discovered that there were a total of 69 churches within the 20-mile radius. I proceeded to formulate a letter introducing myself and informing them that my summer fieldwork involved preaching at different churches. I typed up the letter and met with Deacon Ross and Pastor Walker for their comments and approval. I then addressed the 69 envelopes and mailed the letters immediately. The responses were overwhelming. All I needed were three more preaching engagements at three different churches. I wanted to choose three different churches, so that I would only need two different prepared sermons.

I received so many acceptance offers that I had to refuse most of them because of my time limitation. I sent thank you letters to all 69 churches, even to those who had refused me. In July of that same summer, I met with Rev. Gary, who was the ordained minister every minister had to meet with if ordination in the American Baptist Churches was being considered.

During my first summer fieldwork assignment in 2013, I preached once at MBC, twice at the First Baptist in Sharon, once at First Parish Church in Plymouth, and once at First Baptist Church in Quincy. I had passed out evaluation forms to at least six members of each church for them to complete after I had finished my sermon. The majority of the evaluations were very positive.

I was very grateful to have learned from the completed evaluations that I had made some progress in my preaching techniques and presentation of the gospel messages, although I had not overcome my nervousness. My first sermon was at MBC and had to be recorded, and my last sermon, which was at First Baptist Church in Quincy, had to be recorded. The recordings of my first and last sermons were to be turned in to SoM on my first day back to school in September 2013. In addition, I wrote a comprehensive report of my assignment, which included the initial announcement of it, my surprised reactions to the assignment, doubts, fears, the prayers prayed, and answered prayers, which lead me to the Internet, formulating the letter, meeting with my mentor and pastor, mailing the letters, my written responses to all pastors who responded to my letter, and so forth.

On my first day of my second semester at TABCOM SoM, I submitted my completed summer fieldwork assignment. Several of the SoM students made excuses to Rev. Bardon and Rev. Pappas for not completing their summer fieldwork assignment. I must admit that I was very pleased that I was not one of those students. Approximately a month later, I received rave reviews and positive comments from Rev. Bardon and Rev. Pappas regarding my summer fieldwork assignment. They were very impressed with the creative strategy that I used to accomplish my assignment. The majority of the SOM students had more computer knowledge and skills than I had. Never the less, I was the one who thought of using the Internet to identify potential preaching opportunities. I rejoiced in spirit and in truth because I knew it was God working through me.

Although my second semester at TABCOM SoM was progressing well, I was very unhappy working at TUSDM. There had been drastic changes in the number of students accepted in the incoming class of DMD 2017. All practice coordinators had a substantial increase in the numbers of students assigned to their group practice. Yet, the number of treatment rooms assigned to each group practice had not increased.

Since I was already unhappy working at TUSDM, I interviewed at Boston University Goldman School for Dental Medicine (BUGSDM) the first week of November 2013. I met with Dr. Guarantee, the Executive Dean of BUGSDM, and Dr. Jones, Chair of the Predoctoral Prosthodontics Department.

During my interview with Dr. Jones, I informed her that TUSDM was unaware that I was interviewing at

BUGSDM and I was in very good standing with TUSDM. I continued by saying that although I was very interested in working at BUGSDM, I was unwilling to leave TUSDM unless BUGSDM paid me the salary I requested. Dr. Jones shared that she was very interested that I come to BUGSDM to teach. She was impressed that after graduating from TUSDM, I continued my educational journey and had obtained two master's degrees.

I was hired on the same day I interviewed with Dr. Jones. I returned to TUSDM and gave them my two-week notice, which included six days of accrued vacation time. On November 23, 2013, I started teaching at BUGSDM as an Associate Clinical Professor. At BUGSDM, an Associate Clinical Professor had equal status and salary as an Associate Professor. The only difference between the two was an Associate Professor had published research papers, whereas an Associate Clinical Professor had little or no published research papers. I did not qualify at BUGSDM for the title of an Associate Professor because I only had one published research paper. Dr. Jones advised me to involve myself in more research since there were ample opportunities to do research at BUGSDM. Honestly, I did not reveal to Dr. Jones that I was not interested in doing any research at this juncture of my life since my primary focus was to complete the SoM program and become an ordained minister.

Once I began teaching at BUGSDM, I soon discovered that there would not be a honeymoon year for me. From the onset, each day was very challenging in numerous ways. The responsibilities were overwhelming that were placed on the group practice leaders by the Dean and Executive Dean. And I was one of those group practice leaders. I soon discovered that my current salary was inadequate, although I was earning a six figure annual salary. Many days I felt as if I had stepped out of the frying pan and into the fire.

Initially, during the group practice weekly Wednesday meetings, all of us attempted to address and resolve such issues as shortage of reliable patients, holding dental students accountable to show up to their scheduled appointments, and protocols for patients who do not show for their appointments. Since I had over 17 years of experience in the group practice model, I felt confident that my expertise would be very helpful and instrumental in addressing and resolving these urgent issues. I soon discovered that addressing and resolving these urgent issues were easier said than done.

If I compared the patient population and location of BUGSDM with the patient population and location of TUSDM, these factors would be different as apples and oranges. I became aware of the fact that the majority of dental the patients seeking dental care at BUGSDM were unable to pay for their needed dental treatment; they were those patients who had been dismissed from TUSDM, and those who only wanted dental treatment when they were in pain. Although at the time of their emergency treatment, the dental patients would say that they were interested in routine comprehensive dental care.

Since I had more than 17 years of experience in teaching and in the group practice model at TUSDM, and I had been involved with its design and implementation from 1997 until November 2013, I felt that I was bringing much experience and expertise to BUGSDM. At TUSDM, the practice coordinators were given the authority to formulate all policies and protocols related to dental students and dental patients because we were responsible for the patients receiving the best dental care humanly possible, for the students learning all phases of general dentistry, and for their on-time graduation. The practice coordinators had awesome responsibilities and full authority to address, implement, and resolve all issues involving dental students and dental patients.

The Administration at TUSDM had informed the practice coordinators that we had complete autonomy over all clinic policies and protocols that involved the dental students. I had the authority to block students from the clinic if they violated clinic policies and protocols or to dismiss patients for their lifetime if they failed to keep three scheduled appointments since we required at least 24 hours cancellation notice from all scheduled patients. There were consequences when these clinic policies and protocols were violated, and each practice coordinator had complete autonomy over all clinic policies and protocols. An example of a violation of clinic policies and protocols would be if a dental student failed seating the patient before unwrapping the sterilized dental instruments. Another example a violation of clinic policies and protocols would be if a dental student forgot to wash her/his hands with soap and water before gloving up.

I soon discovered that my 17 years of experience and expertise teaching and in group practice management would not resolve the urgent issues BUGSDM faced, because the group leaders were not given the same authority I had at TUSDM. The group practice leaders at BUGSDM had all of the responsibilities but no authority. There wasn't anything I could do about the patients' finances, the location of BUGSDM, and patients' being untruthful when they were in pain. Every protocol and policies I suggested to address these urgent issues were voided by those with authority.

Therefore, each day became more difficult for me to endure during the first three months. My dental students had more authority than I and they were not even licensed dentists, and they knew it. Those in authority listened to the students' complaints and passed on their grievances to the practice leaders rather than addressing the grievances head on. Those in authority did absolutely nothing to attract patients who could afford their dental care, such as advertising in the local newspapers and providing shuttle buses throughout metropolitan Boston. Those in authority refused to implement any dismissal policies for three failed scheduled appointments. And those in authority also failed to hold dental students accountable whenever they no showed for their patients' appointments.

During one of my group practice meeting with the dental students, two students confronted me with unprofessional behavior and unacceptable language because they did not have the needed procedures for on-time graduation. I was so totally unprepared for their outburst that I was lost for words. I just stood there speechless. My partner was also dumbfounded but managed to end the meeting. I immediately left the room and went into my Director's office, closed the door, and cried. When Dr. Russell, the Director, came into the office, I told him everything. He was unprepared at the moment to advise me. I informed him that I might decide to submit my resignation by next Wednesday. In the meantime, I would not be in work for the next two days.

When I have to make serious decisions, I am not impetuous. On the following Wednesday, I informed Dr. Russell that I would continue working at BUGSDM and focus on performing my job to the best of my abilities, and I would not shoulder anyone else's responsibilities. I continued by saying I was earning one salary at BUGSDM and expected everyone to do their job and earn their salaries.

Therefore, I would continue to smile and concentrate on my job. I did just that. I did not waste my time discussing ways to improve the clinic production, I did not waste time discussing ways to recruit different patient populations, and I did not waste time brainstorming, planning, and implementing policies that would increase patients' show rates and decrease no shows. I left these matters in the hands of those individuals in authority.

I devoted my time teaching my assigned dental students to be thorough in diagnosing problems and formulating treatment plan options for each patient. I taught my assigned dental students how to greet each patient and how to develop rapport with them. I taught my assigned dental students that all patients have choices whether to continue coming for their dental care or to go elsewhere. I taught them how to improve their presentation, and the proper way to end each appointment. My 2014 seniors had a mediocre on-time graduation rate.

I was very pleased to receive the largest merit pay increase in my entire teaching career at the beginning of BUGSDM's 2014 fiscal year. I surmised that BUGSDM's individuals in authority were pleased with me. I continued doing what I was already doing and concentrated on performing my job only.

Every day in 2015 and onward at BUGSDM was replica of the previous ones. Some of my colleagues were becoming weary about their job but did nothing. I, on the other hand, took one day at a time and was grateful to God for another day of surviving BUGSDM. I had made my decision about retiring from teaching all together in two years, and I was just trying to do my best every day. Some days were much harder than others. The only major difference between each year was that each graduating class of my group practice had a slight increase in on time graduation.

Since I had been during very well in TABCOM SoM, I submitted my application to TABCOM's Preparation Ministerial Committee in August of 2015, one month before I began my last semester at the SoM. I was given permission to proceed on the preordination track.

During my last semester at SoM, I attended GCTS for a Polity class since TABCOM SoM did not offer it. I was the only seminary student in the class. Rev. Dr. Scott scheduled all of our two-hour weekly classes in his office. I most definitely received my money's worth for the first time. The disadvantage was that I had to make sure that I had completed all of my reading assignments in advance of the next class, so that I could participate effectively during each class since I was the only student taking Polity.

I graduated from TABCOMSoM on Sunday, November 15, 2015. My graduation was held at MBC. Five of my sisters attended my graduation, which meant only one sister was absent.

My next ordination step was to complete numerous forms for the Career Development for Ministers located in Dedham. Once these forms were received and reviewed, a three-day testing and evaluation was scheduled. Many seminarians could not afford the fee charged for this three-day testing and evaluation and relied on their home churches and scholarships. God had been very generous to me, and so I paid the entire cost of the evaluation myself. I completed the three-day testing and evaluation in late winter of 2016.

The outcome of the testing and evaluation was that I would make an excellent chaplain or pastor of a small church, and I was of sound mind, whole, and healthy. I was very pleased with the outcome.

Then I had to select a mentor for watch care, which was also required in the preordination track. I chose Rev. Dr. Kilpatrick in West Medford in January of 2016. I had met him during my attendance at TABCOM SoM, and he had taught my professional ethics course in the spring of 2015. We agreed to meet for two hours bi-weekly at his church. Rev. Dr. Kilpatrick recommended that I agree to the fast track and I concurred.

My time spent with him was very informative, rewarding, and pleasant. I looked forward to our bi-weekly meetings. Rev. Dr. Kilpatrick had a wealth of God's knowledge, understanding, and wisdom. He was very generous and thoughtful when sharing his faith journey, his experiences as a pastor of several churches, and knowledge of the hierarchical structure of TAMBCOM and American Baptist USA (ABUSA). My watch care was completed in four months, which was the end of April 2016. Rev. Dr. Kilpatrick asked me to preach the traditional Worship Service on Father's Day in June 2016. I accepted his invitation.

I met with the Ministerial Preparation Committee for a second time, which was a continuation of the preordination process. I was asked to leave the room while the Committee made the decision. The Ministerial Preparation approved me to meet with the Ordination Committee.

Rev. Gary was the Chair of the Ordination Committee to discuss my ordination paper. My first two meetings were scheduled in December 2016. I had to read each section and stop for corrections, comments, and suggestions from the Ordination Committee. Each meeting was at least two hours in length. Rev. Gary suggested that Julia meet with me separately before their next meeting, which was scheduled in January 2017, hoping that my ordination paper would be ready for their approval. Julia met with me at our convenience twice. She was very patient with me and prodded me to clarify my thoughts and beliefs. In other words, Julia's proficiency in writing and expertise in the English language, written and spoken, were the main reasons my ordination paper was more readable.

My ordination paper was approved and my ordination defense was four weeks later in March 2017. I appeared to be calm, cool, and collected. I was actually very nervous that Sunday in March while defending my ordination paper. I had to read each session and then stop for questions from all of the delegates present from the different TABCOM's churches. Since TABCOM has more than 300 churches in its organization, the churches were very well represented. Once I finished reading my ordination paper and I had answered all questions, I was requested to vacate the sanctuary while a decision to approve or disapprove me for ordination. My ordination defense included such topics as theology, the Trinity, Jesus, Holy Spirit, God and salvation, and the following paragraphs expressed my beliefs:

My theology is about sharing the goodness of God with as many of God's children as possible. I want to be the salt of the earth by proclaiming Christ's marvelous light to a dying world through my preaching and teaching the good news of Jesus Christ. I am called to be involved in God's public arenas addressing social justice issues that affect God's most vulnerable people by being a voice for the hopeless, voiceless, homeless, jobless, and incarcerated. I believe in devoting my life helping to eliminate unfair and unjust governmental, political, economic, and educational systems through faith-based community organizing. God is able, and with my willing mind, I can help transform God's world to reflect God's marvelous light.

I believe in the Trinity. God is the first of the Trinity. I believe God is the Creator of all humankind and everything. Without God nothing would exist. God existed before time came into being. God is everywhere (omnipresence). God is all-powerful (omnipotent). God is all-knowing (omniscience). There is no one and nothing more loving, powerful, knowledgeable, wiser, generous, understanding, forgiving, merciful, and patient than God. God is complete all by God's self. I believe God loves and cares for me as parents care for their children. Sometimes God is my Mother, and other times God is my Father. I believe God is all spirit and has no physical form. I need a daily relationship with God, with the community of faith, and all of God's children. Therefore, I see God in every person I meet because there is good in everyone.

Jesus is the divine Son of God, the second of the Trinity. Jesus is my Savior and Lord of my life. Jesus is my Redeemer and my closest Friend. Jesus is the heart of my Christian faith. Without Jesus there is no gospel. Jesus was God in the beginning. Jesus and God are one. Being all God and all man, Jesus humbled himself and became obedient to death, leading to his resurrection. Jesus's death and resurrection redeemed me. God raised Jesus to the highest place and raised him above every name. At the name of Jesus, every knee will bow and every tongue confesses that Jesus Christ is Lord to the glory of God.

The Holy Spirit is God's Spirit, third of the Trinity. I believe the Holy Spirit functions as my Sustainer each day. Jesus Christ promised me that I would never be alone. Jesus has been true to his word. The Holy Spirit has comforted and counseled me through all of my trials and tribulations throughout my lifetime. I realize that all of my past hurts and pains have been transformed through the Holy Spirit for the glory of God.

As a result, I have been made whole, healthy, better, stronger, happier, and convinced that in all things and at all times God's Spirit abides in me and with me.

God desired relationship with a living being, and so God created humankind as male and female in God's image and likeness. I believe God revealed God's holy and mighty power through the unconditional and redeeming love demonstrated by Jesus's life, death, and resurrection. For once and for all, sin which leads to death has been defeated by Jesus Christ when Jesus Christ died on the cross and arose from the dead on the third day in possession of all power. My faith tells me, and I know that I have been saved, redeemed, and justified through Jesus's life, death, and resurrection. God has shown me that God is concerned about me 24/7 as I live on earth in my temporal body, and only the things I do for God will last forever.

I believe salvation means an abundant life and freedom in Jesus Christ. Sin had separated humankind from God and this sin grieved God. God still desired relationship with us. God gave God's one and only begotten son, so that whosoever believes in him will not perish but have eternal life. Jesus died on the cross for all past, present, and future sins once and for all. Jesus' blood made a way for all people to have a relationship with the Creator God. Because Jesus Christ redeemed me, I believe Jesus cares for me as a good shepherd cares for his sheep. Since Jesus was tempted, and yet without sin, I know that whenever I am tempted, Jesus sits on the right side of the throne of God, always ready to intercede on my behalf. I have unlimited access to God, and I never have to leave a voice message. God knows my needs, desires, and wants even before I am even aware of them, because God is complete and not lacking any thing. Therefore, I have no lack in any area of my life, because God fulfills my every need.

I believe all Scripture is God-breathed and is useful for teaching, rebuking, correcting, and training in righteousness (2 Timothy 3:16). At one time, God's people did not have the written Word of God. When the Old Testament was first written on scrolls, only the priests were permitted to read God's written Word. God's people had to rely totally on their memories. Two-thirds of the New Testament was written during Apostle Paul's lifetime and inspired by God. I am blessed and fortunate to have God's written Word, and I have followers of Jesus Christ as witnesses to help me obtain Godly understanding and wisdom.

God worked in the lives of individuals during Biblical days, and God still works on my behalf. I do not have any words of my own to save myself or anyone. But I do have God's Word, and God's Word has supernatural power because John 1:1 says, "in the beginning was the Word, and the Word was with God, and the Word was God." I depend on God's Word to direct my life each day. I depend on God's Word to assist me in making decisions. I depend on God's Word to protect me from harm, dangers, and snares. Whenever I am in harm's way, I am depending on God through it all. I have grown to know that there is no fear in God. The only way I can control my fear is to depend more on God. I have grown to know that in all things God works for my good.

I believe, and the Bible supports my belief, that God's call to the church is a call to unity, love, and holiness and that all believers in Jesus Christ will be persuasive witnesses to the world. The church is a community of gathered believers in Jesus Christ by the Holy Spirit. As gathered believers, the church acknowledged Jesus Christ as Lord and the head of the church and is called to be missional people and a worshipping, ministering, and teaching community. Colossians 1:18 says that Jesus is the head of the body, the church. Jesus is the beginning and the first born from among the dead, so that in everything, Jesus might have supremacy.

After about an hour, I was asked to return to the sanctuary and was informed that the delegates had approved me to be ordained into the ministry to preach and teach the gospel of Jesus Christ. I cried tears of joy after hearing the delegates' decision, and I was lost for words. My ordination was scheduled on the calendar for Sunday, May 28th, 2017 at 4:00 PM at MBC. Pastor Walker told me two days later that all of the preparations for my ordination were my responsibility. I requested a list of all of the ministers who were the chairpersons of the different associations in TABCOM, those whom I was unfamiliar with but should be invited. Pastor Walker asked Susan, MBC's secretary, to provide the names and addresses of all of the ministers throughout New England who should be invited to my ordination. It was of no consequences whether those invited accepted my invitations, but it was the appropriate thing to do. Pastor Walker gave me a template of the order of ordination to follow. He informed me that MBC would cover the cost of the ordination dinner in full.

I chose the invitations first and ordered them. Then I sent emails to all of the pastors in TABCOM I wanted to participate in my ordination service. I asked Dr. Rev. Kilpatrick to be the guest preacher to deliver the sermon. I asked Pastor Walker which part for the ordination service he wanted to participate in. Slowly but steadily, I filled in all parts of my ordination service. Many of my SoM professors were invited to participate. There were only three ministers who could not participate due out of town commitments or vacation. May 28th was Memorial Day weekend. Pastor Littleton, my sister-in-law, was a pastor of her church in Mississippi, and she agreed to fly to Massachusetts to participate. Carrie and Cassie promised me that they would be present.

On Sunday, May 28th, 2017, my ordination proceeded without any unforeseen incident. Everyone who had said they would be present showed up. My ordination service was absolutely beautiful. Near the end of the service, all ordained ministers laid hands on me. Then one of them prayed aloud, and I was moved to tears. I was ordained as the Reverend Margaret Jean Howard during my ordination. Then at end of the official ordination service, all of my family members and I stood in a receiving line just like at weddings; everyone came and congratulated me and proceeded to Harris

Hall to share dinner and fellowship. I was too excited to eat a bite.

Cassie had broken her ankle falling down a stairwell in her home the day before she was scheduled to leave to attend my ordination. But her broken ankle did not prevent her from attending to my ordination. Since she and Carrie were only flying in for 24 hours, at my ordination was the first time I laid my eyes on them. They had arrived in Brockton late on Saturday, March 27th, and were scheduled to depart at 8:00 PM on Sunday, March 28th. I knew nothing would prevent Cassie and Carrie from attending my ordination, except hospitalization or death. They had been faithful and supportive of me in all of my endeavors, and I, in turn, had been faithful and supportive of them in theirs.

After arriving home later on Sunday, May 28th, I was totally exhausted. At first I was unable to sleep. But once I did fall asleep, I slept undisturbed the entire night. Upon waking the next morning, I thanked God first. Then I asked God what work did God want me to do? For many years now, thanking God first each morning had become a habit and an act of gratitude.

Over the next few months, I accepted several preaching engagements, which were in Massachusetts,

Alabama, Florida, and Mississippi. Although I felt that I was preaching enough, I had this inner desire to do more of something. My dilemma was that I did not know what this something was.

After the best clinical dental professors in my department decided to resign from BUGSDM during the summer of 2017, by August of the same year, I decided that it was time for BUGSDM and me to part ways. I just didn't enjoy teaching anymore, and I felt that I had no support from the remaining faculty members. I knew I was in no condition to be supportive of anyone because I was too busy watching my back from the Administration. Teaching had become too stressful. The same problems remained but were more alarming. The faculty's moral was at an all times low, including mine. I continued to smile each day but only on the outside. My heart, thoughts, and mind were focused on my future, and BUGSDM and anyone or thing related to BUGSDM were not included. I was looking forward to severing all contacts with BUGSDM. Just the thought lightened my spirit and heart.

After returning from my August 2017 two-week vacation, I submitted my letter of retirement as of March 31st, 2018. With this feat accomplished, I felt much better. I could now concentrate on just getting through each day until March 31st, and each completed day at BUGSDM brought me closer and closer to my retirement. I even checked the number of vacation days I had accrued and the number I would have accrued by March 31st. I decided to routinely schedule vacation days each month so that my tenure at BUGSDM was easier on me, and it was.

However, around the same time, Pastor Walker informed the diaconate in March 2017 that he would be leaving MBC later in 2017. He asked them to keep this information to themselves in the meantime. Robert told me and I promised not to say anything. This was very difficult mainly because I could not express how I felt until Pastor Walker announced his transition from pastoring MBC or tell me personally. I grieved but kept it to myself.

Pastor Walker had decided to leave MBC as pastor and transition back to Dallas, Texas. I was happy for him, yet very sad for me. I had known Pastor Walker for over 30 years. He had been my pastor, confidant, mentor, friend, and father in the ministry. I had always envisioned that I would move back to Alabama while Pastor Walker was still at MBC. It never occurred to me that this would be reversed. Personally, I took his impending departure very hard.

Now, before Pastor Walker left, the diaconate and many members wanted to select another pastor for MBC to avoid being without a settled pastor. I, on the other hand, did not agree. I felt that MBC would be better off to employ an interim pastor during our grieving and transition period. However, since I was an ordained minister, I did not want the members to think I was interested in becoming the interim or settled pastor. Since Robert was a deacon and vice chair of the diaconate, I suggested to him that MBC needed to wait before voting for a settled pastor, because we needed time grieve and decide which direction MBC needed to go. I felt that none of the members were ready to make the right decision about a settled pastor. I knew I was not.

It had been my experience at MBC, the majority of the members had followed those members with the loudest voices, especially when those loud voices had come from men. People with loud voices never have impressed me. Robert was an ordained deacon of the church; he was in good standing, and he had an excellent record of being a person others would listen to.

I believe in talking to God about important decisions first. I had done just that. Deciding on a new settled pastor was an important decision. I had meditated on God's

Word and prayed to God about what the members of MBC should do.

The questions I asked God, "Should we request an interim pastor to be assigned by TABCOM or a settled pastor?" I struggled with God's answer to me for a few months, because God's answer was totally opposite of what the majority of the church members wanted. I thought to myself, how in the world was I supposed to tell the members this news? I knew the Holy Spirit, which is God's Spirit, had told me to advise MBC church body to delay voting on a settled pastor since my only vested interest was doing what was right for the general good of the church body. I said the general good rather than the greater good because the word general good denotes inclusivity and greater good denotes exclusivity or divisions. God is an inclusive God. Therefore, I did not want to incur any harsh objections and confrontational behaviors from any of the members during the fast approaching scheduled church meeting. I don't have thick skin as some people do. My feelings have always gotten hurt when people have treated me unfairly with their harsh words and actions. I know I should have been bold in this matter, but I was not. I failed God, myself, and the church body in this matter by not attending the church meeting. Instead, I had a 'me' day, which I thoroughly enjoyed. First, I went to Planet Fitness and exercised for one hour, and then I went to Star Nails for my manicure and pedicure.

The diaconate and the majority of the membership felt that MBC would be better off with a settled pastor. Since I was aware of the way the majority felt, I did not attend the meeting scheduled. The pain would have been too much for me. Well, a new settled pastor was voted for and MBC had a new settled pastor. MBC's new settled pastor had been a member of the church for 14 years, and prior to becoming an ordained minister, he had been an ordained deacon and had completed ANTS in 2015.

Pastor Walker preached his last sermon on Sunday, October 1, 2017 at MBC. I, in turn, officially began my grieving period immediately. Although Pastor Walker had not died, I felt that I would never see him or Paulette ever again on this side of heaven. I did not envy Pastor Walker and Paulette in any way. It was just that Pastor Walker had been my pastor for many years and he was very important to me.

The new settled pastor was installed on Sunday, October 8, 2017, which was exactly one week after the Pastor

Walker's departure. I attended our 8:00 AM Jazz Worship Service and our 10:45 AM traditional worship service on Sunday, October 8th to show my public support of our new settled pastor. But God knew my true feelings.

I grieved every day for six months. I just went through the motion of fulfilling my responsibilities and obligations. I heart was broken. I was missing Pastor Walker tremendously, but he was not my pastor anymore and it was unfair to him and his family to burdened them with my grief. During my grieving, I told God all about what I was going through, how I felt, and the fact I did not know what to do. Slowly, I began to think about my promise to God concerning helping God's most vulnerable people in some way. I knew this was the Holy Spirit guiding me to think about others and less about myself.

Robert Jr. had asked me to mentor the eighth-grade girls less than a year ago in 2016, because he recognized they were in dire need of someone with a big loving heart. Robert Jr. was a certified math teacher and taught math to eighth-graders. I had gone to Robert Jr.'s classroom twice a year for over ten years as a motivational and inspirational speaker when he taught at the Plouffe Academy. But since he had been at West Middle School, I had only spoken to his class a couple of times.

As I began thinking about the real possibility of mentoring eighth-grade girls on a regular basis, I stopped thinking about myself and how much I missed Pastor Walker. Each morning after exercising, I would spend time writing and formulating a mentoring program for eight-grade girls. I completed the format of the mentoring program by October and presented concept to Mr. Campbell, the Principal of West Middle School, the same month. He was completely on board, and introduced it to the Superintendent of Brockton Public Schools. She also supported me in mentoring the eight-grade girls. Mr. Campbell agreed to take on the responsibility of obtaining parental permission from the eighth-grades girls' parents/guardians each year.

By the end of December 2017, I had founded the Keeping It Real Mentoring Program (KIRMP) for eighth-grade girls. This program would be primarily for eighth-grade girls, but I would be willing to mentor them beyond the eighth-grade, if they desired me to. In my sermon on January 28th, 2018 at MBC during our Jazz Worship Service, I shared how God had redirected my thoughts from me to others, which resulted in me founding the KIRMP for eighth-grade girls and beyond during my grieving period. And it worked!

I had implemented the KIRMP earlier in January 2018 at the West Junior Middle School located on West Street in Brockton. The mentoring sessions were held on the second and fourth Mondays of each month beginning at 2:35 PM. My focus has been to help develop self-esteem, cultivate wholesome and healthy attitudes, and motivate and inspire great expectations by doing their best in school and out of school, to use their free time wisely, become leaders and not followers, to be producers and not consumers, etc.

My last day at BUGSDM was on Wednesday, March 21, 2018. I decided to use some of my accrued vacation days for the remaining days in March. I felt free for the first time in 63 years. BUGSDM would pay me for all remaining unused vacation days and did.

Since I had been busy throughout my married life pursuing one college degree after another, Robert and Robert Jr. were sure that, in a matter of months after my retirement, I would be informing them about another long-term degree program I was interested in taking. To their surprise and mine, I have had no desire to commit to any long-term advanced degree program, even if many are accessible online. After 63 years of working and striving to fulfill my educational and professional goals, my insatiable thirst for more knowledge had now been satisfied. I am ready and deserve to lead a less active and demanding life.

Reflecting back over my life, I was enrolled in business courses in my late teens, attending Forsyth and Northeastern in my twenties, enrolled as a dental student in my early thirties, pursuing a Master of Education degree in my forties, completing a Master of Public Health in my fifties, and completing a certificate program in Professional Ministry in my sixties.

Although I had decided that I do not aspire to attend any long-term educational program, I am staying active doing only the things I enjoy. In June 2018, Mr. Campbell, the principal of West Junior Middle School, held their first annual breakfast for the graduating eighth-graders. He invited me to speak at this breakfast, which was scheduled at 9:00 AM. As I walked into the school's auditorium that morning, I received a standing ovation from the students. Of the four individuals asked to speak, I was the only one who was not a paid employee of the Brockton Public Schools. In other words, I was the only one from the community present. It was an honor to be invited an appreciated. This was an example of God using me to do God's will God's way.

After more than 37 years in the dental profession, I am venturing into an area of professional ministry that has stimulated my mind with exciting possibilities and challenges. I am absolutely thrilled with the way and direction my twilight years are headed.

Every day I thank God first for life and freedom in Jesus Christ. Because of God's love grace and mercy each day, I am still living on this side of heaven. For the first time, I have control of my schedule. I don't have to concern myself with the commuter train schedules, whether dental patients show or not show for their appointments, whether the students show for the patients appointments, whether dental students have all of their needed clinic procedures, and whether the dental students diligently work hard to complete those procedures already treatment planned, to name a few. I am free indeed from all of those issues, and the salary BUGSDM paid me was not worth all of the aggravation. A peace of mind and excellent health should not be taken for granted, and I do not. Life is good, and I thank God for everything.

Since I am retired and have opportunities to enjoy my golden years, I reflect back over my life and I am in awe of where God has brought me from and through. I remember those long hot and humid days working in the fields from the age of seven; I remember the great fear I had of snakes, and I remember those hot and humid days when I could never clench my thirst for more water. I remember wishing that I could live a different life and wear beautiful clothes. I remember being ashamed of the houses I lived in and our furniture. I remember wishing that Cassie and I shared a bedroom together rather than all of the girls in one bedroom. Also, I remember wishing that I had a twin bed all to myself rather than having three in a bed.

I remember those challenging years of my young adult life and those awful jobs I had. I remember those horrendous furnished apartments I had lived in and those long bus rides to and from work. I remember waiting in the snow for those buses with Angela in my arms on those cold wintery days. Now, Angela is a lawyer and has two law degrees. I remember these challenges as if they were yesterday.

Yet, I don't sit around every day merely reminiscing about the past, because God still has much work for me to do. Yet, every now and then, I do pause and do some reflecting. God has been very generous and loving to me. Everything I experienced was for my good and made me stronger and better. I was taught to do good deeds and be a blessing, so others will be a blessing me. Mama was a fifth-grade scholar and Daddy was a fourth-grade scholar, as I shared before, yet both of them were full of God's wisdom. They did not have much in the way of money, real estate, investments or any material things. But their possessions were much more valuable. They were full of God's love and wisdom.

As I child, I did not appreciate Mama and Daddy, and rarely did I have good thoughts about them. Many times I thought they were mean and hateful. I questioned why they had so many children since they could not afford them. I was even bold enough to ask this question to Daddy one day after I was living on my own. Daddy asked me which one of his children should he have left out, maybe Margaret? I thought about Daddy's profound response to my question. I quickly apologized to Daddy for my ignorance and questioning God's blessings and his and Mama's business. Besides, if Mama and Daddy did not have 18 children, I might not have ever been born. This was not the first time I had put my foot in my mouth, and it was definitely not the last.

As long as I have breath, I will continue to preach and teach the gospel of Jesus Christ and mentor God's most vulnerable people, especially young girls, to dream big and work as hard as if their lives depended on it to reach their fullest potential in life. Otherwise, I remain open to all that God has for me.

This is the beginning of the 2019 school and the beginning of the third year for KIRMP at West Middle School. I am just as excited about the possibilities and opportunities available to my eighth-grade girls as if they were my own biological ones.

I met with Mr. Campbell at West Junior High School on September 16th. Our meeting was very rewarding, enjoyable, and filled with great expectations. Once the meeting ended, I requested permission to stop by my son's classroom to introduce myself to the eighth-grade class. Kindly and thoughtfully, my son permitted me to speak for a few minutes announcing the KIRMP for eighth-grade girls offered every second and fourth Mondays of each month according to their school schedule.

I have been invited to speak on October 24th at 9:00 AM at the Eighth-Grade Girls Tea at West Middle School. Because of the KIRMP, the educators at West Middle School and principal are providing opportunities for all eighth-graders to be exposed to my presentations earlier in the school. I have complete faith that this will result in greater increase in attendance at KIRMP's bi-weekly mentoring sessions because with God, all things are possible. According to the comments from the teachers at West Middle School, they would like for all of the eighth-graders to attend my presentation at the beginning of school and in January of each year in order to help keep the eighth-graders motivated, inspired, and interested in doing their best each day.

As I continue my retirement from the dental profession, which I do not miss at all, I feel freer than I have ever felt. Since the age of seven, I felt that I had to schedule specific tasks to do each day because if I did not, there was no else to complete these tasks for me. When I was working, I had to be at the gym at a specific time, then shower so that I could catch the commuter rail at a specific time each workday. In addition, I had to leave home on weekends to arrive to church on time each Sunday and midweek for Bible study, whether I was the teacher or an attendee. I went to the supermarket at a specific time so that I would not get caught up waiting in the checkouts lines for extended periods of time.

Retirement for me is being free from a regimented schedule from day to day. I no longer have to catch a commuter rail, and therefore, I do not show up at the gym at the same time each morning. And I am very flexible when it comes to going to the supermarket. The things I have control over, I have totally taken control over them. And the things I have no control over, I just go with the flow.

As I look toward my future, I know that my life's journey will still present some challenges for me. As a matter of fact, I was given a challenge to live with on November 1, 2019 concerning my recent bone density results. On October 24, 2019, I had an annual physical examination with my primary care physician (PCP). I had fasted so that my blood was drawn on the same day. It had been six years since I had a bone densitometry. Therefore, I was scheduled for a bone densitometry on October 30, 2019.

For 72 years, I have been disease-free. I have had my share of colds, flus, and strep throats. Now it is my turn to live with a chronic disease. On November 1, 2019, I was told that I have osteoporosis, and I needed to begin treatment for it. Calmly, I scheduled an appointment for Wednesday, November 13th at 8:30 AM. I could have scheduled my appointment earlier, but I chose November 13th because I needed time to talk to God and do so research on osteoporosis.

During this time, my thoughts wondered on my lack of boldness in sharing the message the Holy Spirit had given me in 2017 regarding MBC needing an interim pastor rather than a settled one. I was not pleased with my behavior, and I knew God was not pleased either. On Sunday, November 3, 2019, I stood before the MBC's members and confessed my disobedience to God when I failed to attend the church meeting in August 2017. I did not make any excuses for myself and I asked the members to forgive me. Although the outcome of the votes could have been the same, that did not excuse my disobedience to God and my failure to MBC's members. Afterwards, I knew God had given me a clean heart and had renewed my spirit in Jesus Christ.

From my limited knowledge about osteoporosis, I knew that there was no cure for this aging disease. And I began to wonder whether I was at low, moderate, or high risk for fractures. Every tragic thing a person could imagine ran through my mind all at once for a few minutes. So, I closed my eyes and began slow deep breathing exercises. After a few minutes had passed, I began to think about God, who God was, who God is, and who God will always be. I told myself that God already knew I had osteoporosis long before I had the bone densitometry done. So, I talked to God about my concerns, which were many. I told God that I was very grateful for these 72 years of excellent health, and I needed God's help in order for me live a victorious life with osteoporosis, because only God can do this for me. With God I can do all things through Jesus Christ who strengthens me, and I cannot do anything without God.

I saw my PCP on November 13th as planned. I was told that I had lost only three percent of my bone density; I was at low risk for fractures and I was prescribed Fosamax. All of this information was good news to me. As it turned out, I had been doing the correct exercises regularly for many years, which strengthen my bones and muscles. I was very pleased to learn that I could continue these exercises without risking doing damage to my bones. I have been very dedicated doing squats and working out on the elliptical and treadmill machines.

Living with osteoporosis is just another phase of life I am meant to live with, and I intend to live my life to its fullest. I told God many years ago that I wanted a complete life in God, and I desired everything God had for me. To date, I have not changed my mind. Although my life has not been a crystal stair, I remain thankful to

God for everything. God still has much work and blessings just for me…Margaret Jean Howard. Thank God!

God is always true to God's Word, because God never lies. God always saves the best for the last, and I am living God's best for me right now. I believe my life is going to continue to get better and better as I become older and older.

As I remain a work in progress, I will not reach perfection until I am just like God. Right now, I am just thankful to God for my life's journey, which includes the good, bad, and ugly, because God has remained with me through it all. I know that in all things, God works for the good of Margaret, who loves God, who has been called according to God's purpose. All praises and glory belong to God.